CONTENTS

ACKNOWLEDGMENTS

Special thanks to the teachers who allowed me to teach lessons in their classrooms.
Dinah Brown, Palmquist Elementary School, Oceanside, CA
Laura Chandler, Richland Elementary School, San Marcos, CA
Pat Feist, Laurel Elementary School, Oceanside, CA
Linda Lowe, Richland Elementary School, San Marcos, CA
Lawrence Pallant, Laurel Elementary School, Oceanside, CA
Patti Reynolds, Paloma Elementary School, San Marcos, CA
Leslie Robinson, Laurel Elementary School, Oceanside, CA
Carol Schurlock, Knob Hill Elementary School, San Marcos, CA
Carole Smith, Palmquist Elementary School, Oceanside, CA
John Swaim, Palmquist Elementary School, Oceanside, CA

Special thanks to those teachers who contributed their insights and expertise by sharing their classroom experiences with me.
Caren Holtzman, Laurel Elementary School, Oceanside, CA
Patty Montgomery, Pacifica Elementary School, Oceanside, CA
Shelley Ferguson, East Lake Elementary School, Chula Vista, CA
Suzanne McGrath, East Lake Elementary School, Chula Vista, CA
Maryann Wickett, Paloma Elementary School, San Marcos, CA
Juli Tracy, Laurel Elementary School, Oceanside, CA
Pam Long, North Terrace Elementary School, Oceanside, CA

Thanks also to those people who helped me make this book a reality.
To Marilyn Burns, who gave me encouragement, critical feedback, and guidance. Without her, this book would not have been possible.

To Stephanie Sheffield, who gave me support and feedback during the entire writing process.

To Maryann Wickett, who was there every step of the way, listening to me and encouraging me.

To Annette Raphel, whose ideas are behind many of the activities in this book.

To Lorri Ungaretti for her caring and persistent editorial assistance.

To Caren, Michelle, Alberto, Peter, Tom, and Stephanie for their friendship.

To my parents for supporting me in my education.

To the people at the White Rabbit Bookstore, La Jolla, CA, for their help in searching for children's books.

To Math Solutions consultants for sharing their wisdom and friendship.

MATH
AND
LITERATURE
(Grades 4–6)

by Rusty Bresser
Introduction by Marilyn Burns

MATH SOLUTIONS PUBLICATIONS

Editorial direction by Lorri Ungaretti
Art direction and design by Aileen Friedman
Page layout by David Healy

Printed in the United States of America on recycled paper.

ISBN 0-941355-14-4

Distributed by Cuisenaire Company of America, Inc.
P.O. Box 5026
White Plains, NY 10602-5026
(800) 237-3142

Marilyn Burns Education Associates is dedicated to improving mathematics education. For
information about Math Solutions courses, resource materials, and services, write or call:
Marilyn Burns Education Associates
150 Gate 5 Road, Suite 101
Sausalito, CA 94965
Telephone (415) 332-4181
Fax (415) 331-1931

INTRODUCTION

After publishing our first *Math and Literature* book for teachers in kindergarten through grade 3, we began to receive requests from teachers in grades 4 through 6 for a similar resource. After publishing our second *Math and Literature* book, again for the primary grades, the requests from upper-grade teachers increased. Rusty Bresser had contributed to part of *Math and Literature (K-3), Book Two,* by Stephanie Sheffield, and he agreed to take on the challenge for writing a version for grades 4 through 6.

For more than a year, Rusty searched for books to use as springboards for mathematics lessons. He tried lessons in a variety of classes and had colleagues also try them so that he could compare notes from different classes. He worked during evenings and weekends, writing about the lessons and sorting through student work. He'd send me drafts of his descriptions of what happened and samples of what the students did, and he and I had many discussions about all aspects of the lessons, including how some things might have been handled differently and what else he might have asked students to do. Rusty often returned to classes to extend activities or refine lessons. He worked tirelessly.

In the end, Rusty chose to include lessons based on 20 children's books. Each lesson is presented as a vignette of what actually occurred with students, accompanied by samples of student work to illustrate how the students responded.

Rusty is well qualified to write this book. For the past 10 years, he has been a classroom teacher at Laurel Elementary School in the Oceanside Unified School District in Oceanside, California. His classroom experience with grades 3 through 6 has given him a good deal of experience working with intermediate students. In addition, Rusty's inservice experience as an instructor of the Math Solutions summer courses, as a workshop leader for the California State Department of Education and the San Diego County Office of Education, and as an instructor at the San Diego Extension of the University of California has given him a firm sense of teachers' needs and interests.

The reading level of the children's books Rusty chose varies. Some are picture books geared for younger children. However, Rusty, and the other teachers who also tried the lessons, found that the simpler books often led to mathematical investigations of suitable complexity for older students. Also, the fourth through sixth graders enjoyed being read to and were engaged by the books Rusty chose.

Rusty's dedication in writing this book has been impressive. He has created something that has a firm basis in the realities of classroom instruction and that responds to the current standards for teaching mathematics. I was constantly stimulated by my work with Rusty on this book, and I feel that I learned new things that have served me in working with students. I'm pleased and proud to present this book to elementary teachers searching for ways to help students think, reason, and solve mathematical problems.

Marilyn Burns
May 1995

Annabelle Swift, Kindergartner

In *Annabelle Swift, Kindergartner*, by Amy Schwartz, Annabelle faces her first day of kindergarten. Armed with (poor) advice from her older sister, she seems to say all the wrong things. After the kindergartners turn in 6 cents each for milk, they begin to count how much they have altogether. The other children give up at around 10 cents, but Annabelle counts all the way to $1.08, impressing everyone in the room. The teacher appoints Annabelle milk monitor, and she goes to the school kitchen to collect the milk cartons. Using the information in the book, students figure out how many cartons of milk were purchased. They later work together to solve problems about buying milk for their own class.

materials: none

"**D**o any of you have a younger brother or sister?" I asked Leslie Robinson's fourth grade class.

Many hands shot up in the air.

"Do any of you have a brother or a sister who is in kindergarten?" I asked them. This time, a few students' hands went up.

"What was it like for your brother or sister on the first day of kindergarten?" I asked.

"My brother cried," said Julio.

"My sister cried till she got there, then she didn't want to go home," added Antoinette.

"Raise your hand if you remember your first day in kindergarten," I said. Nearly all the students raised their hands, giggling and whispering to one another.

"I remember my first day in kindergarten and that was a long, long time ago. I remember that I cried, and my sister had to hold my hand," I said.

Everyone laughed.

"Today I want to share with you a book that's about a kindergartner's first day in school," I said. "Her name is Annabelle, and she has an older sister who's in third grade. But since you're in the fourth grade, let's pretend that her older sister is a fourth grader."

The class listened attentively as I read the story. The students enjoyed hearing Annabelle's older sister, Lucy, teach Annabelle all the "fancy stuff" in preparation for her first day in school. They giggled when Lucy told

Annabelle to "ask lots of questions because teachers like that." They were happy for Annabelle when she showed her teacher how smart she was by counting all the children's milk money.

"How much money did Annabelle count?" I asked.

"One hundred and eight!" responded the students.

"One hundred and eight what?" I asked.

"One hundred and eight cents!" they answered.

On the board, I wrote:

108 cents

"This is one way to write the total amount of milk money. Does anyone know another way I could write it?" I asked.

"You could write 1 dollar and 8 cents," suggested Bethany. I wrote on the board:

$1.08

"How much did each carton of milk cost?" I asked. The students remembered that each kindergartner pulled out a nickel and a penny.

"Six cents," they chorused.

I continued reading the story. I reached the part where Annabelle's teacher, Mr. Blum, congratulates Annabelle for having counted all the money and then asks her to take the milk money to the cafeteria. I stopped reading and asked the class a question.

"If Annabelle took $1.08 to the cafeteria, and each milk costs 6 cents, how many milks did Annabelle bring back? How could you solve this problem?" I asked.

"You could draw a bunch of milks and put a 6 on top of each one. Then you could add all the 6s until you get to $1.08. Then count the milks," suggested Daryl. I wrote on the board:

Draw milks.

"Does anyone have another idea?" I asked.

"You could guess how many kids are in Annabelle's class," said Martin. "Then divide $1.08 by that number." I recorded Martin's idea on the board:

Guess and divide to check.

"Does anyone have another idea?" I asked again. I find that if I keep asking for additional ideas, children get the notion that there are many ways to solve problems. I called on Jack.

"I think that 108 times 6 will equal the number of milks," he said.

"That would be way too many!" Dara declared.

"I'm going to write down all your ideas," I said. "Listen, and then you can try them out later to see if they work." As the students offered suggestions, I recorded them on the board.

"You could use tally marks," said Antoinette.

"How would you use them?" I asked.

"You could circle six tallies at a time 'til you get to 108," she said.

"Then what?" I pushed Antoinette to elaborate further.

"Then I guess you'd have to count the tallies . . . no, the circles," she said, suddenly uncertain. "Yes, you'd count the circles."

"Any other ideas?" I asked.

"I would count by 6s 'til I got to 108," offered Lea.

"How about using a calculator?" suggested Bethany.

"How would you use it?" I asked.

"You could use it to add 6s, like Lea said," Bethany explained.

"Does anyone have another way?" I asked.

"Start at 108 and subtract 6 at a time until you get to zero," said Rolf.

"Now I'd like you to solve the problem with any one of these methods. Just be sure to choose one that makes sense to you," I said. "Or you can use a method that's different from the ones I listed on the board. But be sure to explain your solution using words and numbers."

The final list on the board looked like this:

> *Draw milks.*
> *Guess and divide to check.*
> *Multiply.*
> *Use tally marks.*
> *Count by 6s.*
> *Use a calculator.*
> *Start at 108 and subtract.*

The students went to work immediately. Most seemed to know which method to use to solve the problem and started to write. Others read the ideas I had written on the board to decide which one to use.

When I approached Martin, he was starting to divide 108 by 6.

"Explain to me why you're writing 108 divided by 6, Martin," I said.

"I know it's a division problem. I'm not sure why I know that, but that's what I think," he answered.

Bethany waved me over and asked me to listen to her read what she had written. She read: *"I solved this problem by making tally mark in groups of six to get the sum. The number I got was 18 milks Annabelle gets because theirs 18 kids in her class, and 18 times 6 is $1.08."*

Nichelle drew pictures of milk cartons with six tally marks in each, and she then wrote the number 6 above each carton.

"How did you know to draw 18 milk cartons?" I asked her.

"I kept trying different numbers of milk cartons until it came to $1.08," she explained. "What I did was count the 5s in each box. Then I went back and counted the 1s." She had written: *Because 18 × 5 = 90 + 18 ones = 108 in all.* When I asked Nichelle why she counted the 5s first, she said, "5s are more friendly than 6s."

When I got back to Martin's table, he was just finishing his work.

"How's it going, Martin?" I asked.

"Good! What I did was, I started with 108 and I subtracted 6 each time 'til I got to zero, and I did this 18 times," he explained. "But I wanted to check my work so I added 18 six times and I got 108, so I know I'm right."

How many milks did Annabelle get for $1.08.?

Milk is 6¢ each.

6 6 6 6 6 6 6 6 6 6 6 6

6 6 6 6 6 6

$$18 \text{ children} \times 6 \text{ cents each} = \$1\ 08$$

$$90 + 18 = 108$$

I got the answer by counting the fives in each box and going back and counting the ones. Because 18 × 5 = 90 + 18 ones = 108. in all.

5 × 25 = 125 • 5 people and 25¢ for each milk equals 125¢.

Nichelle multiplied 18 × 5, then went back and added the 1s.

"I have a question," asked Erin. "Is it okay if I just used words and not numbers to explain my answer?"

"It's okay if the words explain your solution and how you got it," I said. "Why don't you read your paper to me?"

Erin read: *"Ten kids would have to pay 60 cents and 20 kids would have to pay $1.20, but $1.08 is 12 cents less than that, which is two kids less so that would be 18 kids and that would be 18 milks!"*

"That makes perfect sense to me," I told her. "But I don't understand why you said you used just words and not numbers. There are lots of numbers in your explanation." I pointed out the numbers.

Erin looked at me with surprise. "But I didn't add or multiply or anything with the numbers," she said.

"How did you figure that 10 kids would have to pay 60 cents?" I asked.

"I did it in my head," Erin answered.

"What did you do in your head?" I asked.

Erin responded, "I did 10 times 6 . . . oops! I guess I did multiply, but I just didn't write it down regular." Because she hadn't done traditional arithmetic, Erin thought that she hadn't used numbers.

"Calculating in your head certainly counts for using numbers," I said. "And your explanation makes good sense to me."

Rolf ran up to me and said excitedly, "I've got the answer!" I followed him back to his seat and listened carefully as he explained.

"I got my answer by subtracting by 6 until I got zero and the answer is 18 milks Annabelle got from the lady!" Rolf exclaimed. He proudly showed me the milks he had drawn in the corner of his paper.

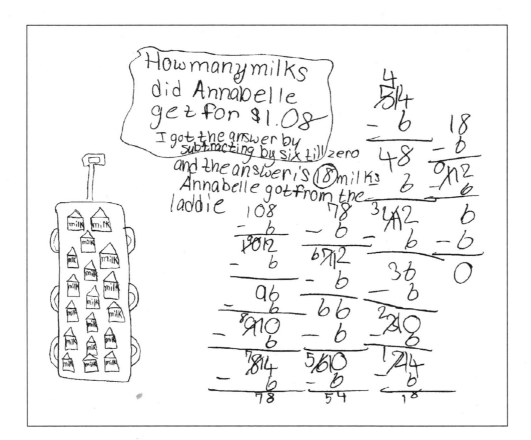

Rolf used repeated subtraction to solve the milk problem.

When all of the children had finished working on the problem, I asked for their attention. "How many milks do you think Annabelle brought back from the cafeteria?" I asked.

"Eighteen!" everyone responded.

"Are you sure?" I asked. This question made a few students uneasy, and I could tell by the looks on their faces that they were wondering if the answer really was 18.

"I want to read the rest of the book to make sure you're all correct," I said. The end of the book revealed the answer. The children applauded when I read the part where the lady in the cafeteria handed Annabelle 18 little cartons of milk and 18 straws.

A Second Problem

"Does anyone know how much it costs to buy a milk in our school cafeteria?" I asked.

"Twenty-five cents," several students volunteered.

"Figure out how much it would cost if everyone at your table bought milks today," I said. "Talk to the people at your table, and raise your hands when you have an answer."

After a few minutes, most hands were wiggling in the air. "What did you find out?" I asked.

"It would cost our table $1.00. We counted by 25s. There are four people at our table, so that's a dollar," reported Ramon.

"We figured it like there was a quarter for each person. We came up with 75 cents for the three of us," said Marcia.

"We know that 25 times 4 is a dollar. That's how we got it," said Jack.

"Four people equals $1.00, and two more would be $1.50," explained Bethany, who was seated at a table of six children.

"Who can predict what my next mathematical question will be?" I asked.

Many hands shot up. "How much would it cost for our whole class to buy milk?" guessed Antoinette.

"That's right. I want you to figure that out and explain your thinking using words and numbers. You can draw pictures if you want," I instructed.

As the students started working, I noticed that they were all trying to count the number of people in the room. I stopped them and asked for their attention.

"What do you need to know in order to solve this problem?" I asked.

"How many students there are," Daryl said.

"I'll give you that information. One person is absent, so 27 students are here today," I reported.

Antoinette made a chart for the six tables. She wrote: *I counted all the tables. Then I counted a quarter for each person and I put the money under the table number and then I added all the money together.*

Daryl got the answer by putting the number 25 on top of a drawing of each person. He then added all the numbers to get the answer.

Martin explained his thinking in writing: *I got $6.75 because 1 × 27 × 25 = 6.75 but to get that anser I added 10 25s and got 250. Then I added 250 + 250 and got 500. Then added eight 25s and got 175. Then added 500 + 175 = 675.*

Nichelle used tally marks to solve the problem. She wrote: *If you make tallies it will be easy. But only if you count them when you're done.*

Jana kept a running total to get her answer. She made a long vertical list from 1 to 27, showing the cumulative total after each number of milks.

Hart added groups of four 25s to get $1.00. First he recorded 25 cents too many times, but he erased the extras. He added up all the dollars and then added together the three extra 25s to get $6.75.

When the students were finished, they took turns sharing how they had arrived at the answer. This is an important part of the lesson, as the students

Hart figured the totals for each table, then added to find the total for all 27 students.

hear the different ways their peers solve the problem. Hearing other solutions can reinforce for students what they already know and help them learn an easier or different way to find the solution.

When we finished our discussion, Julio raised his hand and asked, "Well, aren't we going to get milks for doing all this work?"

"If you have a quarter," I replied.

Jana kept a running tally.

From a Sixth Grade Class

I decided to try the same problem with Laura Chandler's sixth graders. However, I was interested in learning how the students would tackle the problem mentally, without using paper and pencil. Too often, students focus on paper-and-pencil computation and don't get sufficient experience and practice with thinking about numbers and reasoning in their heads.

Before reading the book, I talked with the students about what it was like to have younger brothers and sisters. Some of them loved having younger siblings, and some thought it was "a pain." Most of the students remembered what it was like being a kindergartner on the very first day of school.

The class was completely attentive as I read. When I finished reading the part where Annabelle walks to the cafeteria, I stopped.

"I have a mathematical question," I said. "How many milks did Annabelle bring back to the class? In other words, how many milks did Annabelle buy for $1.08?" A few students raised their hands excitedly.

"Wait just a minute," I said. "I want you to solve this problem in a special way. I want you to promise me something. Please raise your right hand and repeat after me." The students all raised their hands.

"I will not use a pencil or paper to solve this problem," I said in a serious voice. The students repeated the pledge, giggling as they spoke.

"You may discuss the problem with the people at your table, but remember not to use paper or pencil," I told them.

"Can we use a calculator?" asked Cord.

"For today's problem, I want you to solve it mentally," I said. "It's important that you learn to reason with numbers in as many ways as possible, and one of those ways is to figure in your head." I said this because I think that it's valuable for students to understand the purpose of their assignments.

The students spent about 5 minutes sharing their ideas in small groups. When they finished their discussions, I asked for their attention.

"Would anyone like to explain how you solved the problem?" I asked.

"I counted the people in the book," Keir said, with a wry smile on his face. I couldn't tell if he were joking or if he really had counted the children in Annabelle's class when I showed the picture from the book.

"Let's say you weren't able to see the picture and count the kids in the class. How else might you solve the problem, Keir?" I asked.

"You could count by 6s until you get to $1.08," he replied.

"I estimated," said Enzo.

"Tell us how you estimated," I said.

"I guessed 17 and multiplied 17 times 6 and I got 102. That was too small, so I made it 18 times 6 and I got 108," he explained.

"I thought of the problem in my head like a division problem," Cord said. "For example, $1.08 divided by 6 cents is 18. All you do is think '6 goes into 10 one time. And 10 minus 6 equals 4, so you bring down the 8. Then 6 goes into 48 eight times.' Your answer is 18."

"I multiplied 6 and 10," explained Cassie. "I got 60, so I did 60 times 2. From 60 times 2 I got 120. I knew that was too big, so I did 120 minus 108. I got 12 and that is two milks. Now I have 18 milks."

"Is there another way you could solve the problem?" I asked.

"You could start with 108 and keep subtracting 6, but that would take a long time," said Charlene.

"I kind of drew a picture of a division problem in my head," Terell offered. "It looked like a regular old division problem. I could see it in my head and I pretended to use a pencil to divide the numbers."

"I started with 6 times 12 as a guess and that was 72, and it wasn't enough," explained Trina. "So I kept going up, like 6 times 13, 6 times 14, until I got to 6 times 18."

"Now that you've solved the problem mentally, explain in writing exactly what you did to get your answer," I instructed.

When the students finished writing their explanations, I asked them to hand in their papers. "Aren't you going to finish the story?" asked Marcia.

"Do you want to hear it?" I asked.

"Yes!" they all responded. Here was a group of very sophisticated sixth graders, begging me to finish *Annabelle Swift, Kindergartner.* It made my day!

Cassie used estimation, multiplication, and subtraction to solve the milk problem.

Anno's Magic Seeds

In *Anno's Magic Seeds,* by Mitsumasa Anno, a wizard gives Jack two mysterious seeds. The wizard tells Jack that if he bakes and eats one seed, he won't be hungry for a year, and if he buries the other seed, he'll get two new seeds. Jack repeats this process for 7 years, then decides to plant both seeds and find something else to eat for a year. The following year he has four seeds. He eats one and buries the other three. The story continues, with the process changing from time to time. This story leads to an activity in which students search for patterns to determine how many seeds Jack gets over 10 years, then use their patterns to think about how to predict the number of seeds after longer periods of time.

After I'd read just a few pages of Anno's Magic Seeds to Carole Smith's fourth and fifth graders, Calie had a comment.

"I notice a pattern!" she exclaimed.

"Describe the pattern you notice," I said.

"Each year Jack eats one seed, plants one, and gets two magic seeds the following year," Calie explained.

"He's doing the same thing each year," said Flint.

"Does anyone else notice a pattern?" I asked.

"Eats one, plants one, gets two, eats one, plants one, gets two," said Deirdre. "It's a repeating pattern." Others nodded their agreement.

I continued with the story, reading up to the part where Jack realizes that by eating one seed and planting the other, he will continue to get two seeds over and over.

"Jack is going to do something different with the seeds this time," I told the class. "Raise your hand if you have a guess about what he might do next." Many hands shot up. I called on Jansen.

"I think he'll plant both of them," he guessed.

"He might eat both of them," said Deirdre.

"I think he might store them in case there's no food later on," Emily said.

As I read on, the students learned that Jack plants both of the seeds, hoping to get through the winter by eating something different that year.

"Raise your hand if you have a guess about what happened the following year after Jack planted both seeds," I said.

"I think he'll get four seeds," Dylan guessed.

"I think he'll forget about the seeds, and he won't have anything left," said Bernardo. "That would be sad."

After the children made their predictions, I read: "In the spring, two sprouts came up, and in the fall, four seeds were produced. In the winter, Jack baked and ate one seed and buried the other three seeds in the ground."

"How many seeds do you think Jack will get the following year?" I asked.

"Six!" students chorused.

I continued with the story, confirming that they were right and reading that in this second year, Jack eats one seed and plants the other five. The next few pages of the book describe how many seeds are eaten, how many are planted, and how many grow each subsequent year. Again, the students began to notice a pattern in the story.

"There's a different pattern happening now," Judy said. "However many seeds he plants, he then gets double that amount the following year."

"Every time he plants he gets double that, then he eats one, then plants the rest, and gets double that, and so on," explained Dylan.

"It goes 2 times 2 minus 1 equals 3," said Jo. "Then it goes 3 times 2 minus 1 equals 5, and so on."

"The number of seeds is doubling each time, then Jack eats one," said Maggie.

"How is this pattern different from the first pattern?" I asked.

"The first pattern was a repeating pattern and this pattern grows," said Judy.

"At the end of the third year after Jack got the idea of burying both seeds, he gets 10 seeds," I said. "How many seeds do you think Jack will have at the end of the tenth year? Talk to someone next to you and come up with an estimate." After a minute, I repeated my question and called on volunteers.

"I think he'll have 18 seeds," said Tano.

"Why do you think that?" I asked.

"Because 9 times 2 equals 18," he said.

"Why are you using the number 9?" I asked him.

"Because 10 years subtract 1 for the one he ate times 2 because the number of seeds doubles," he explained.

Tano knew that the seeds doubled and that he needed to subtract 1 somewhere, but he had only partial understanding of the problem at this point. I didn't correct him because I knew that he would soon have a chance to explore the problem further. Also, I was interested in hearing what others were thinking. Listening to the students' initial estimates without correcting them gave me a chance to assess their thinking.

"We calculated that he'll have 68 seeds after the tenth year," said Paige. "Because after the third year, he had 10. Then he ate 1 and buried 9, and the seeds doubled. Then he got 18 and he ate 1, and he buried 17. We kept going. We're not really sure, though."

"How might you figure it out to be sure about how many seeds Jack will have at the end of the tenth year?" I asked.

"You could make a graph," said Deirdre.

"You could make a chart," suggested Jed. "I'd make a chart with columns—one column for the years, one for the seeds planted, one for the seeds he got, and one for the seeds eaten."

"You could just write it out using numbers and words," said Calie.

When all the students had shared their ideas, they began to work on the problem. Students organized themselves in various ways. Some chose to work alone, while others formed groups of two, three, or four. Each student, however, recorded on his or her own paper.

Calie solved the problem by writing sentences with numbers and words. She wrote: *1st he plants two and he gets 4 he eats 1 he gets 3. 2nd he plants three and he gets six he eats 1 he get 5. 3rd he plants 5 and he get 10 he eats 1 he get 9.* She finished with the tenth year: *he plants 513 and he gets 1,026 he eats 1 he gets 1,025.*

"How did you figure out how many seeds he gets each time?" I asked.

"I used mental math," she replied.

"Explain how you used mental math, Calie," I probed.

"I doubled each number in my head and subtracted 1 each time," she explained. "Like double 2 is 4, minus 1 equals 3. Then double 3 is 6, minus 1 equals 5. When I got to the big numbers I did double 33 is 66, minus 1 equals 65 and double 513 is 1,026. I knew that 500 plus 500 equals 1,000, and double 13 is 26."

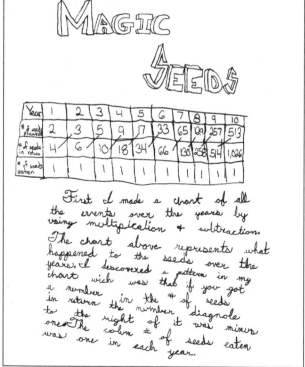

Calie used mental math to double the number of seeds, then subtracted the one that Jack ate.

Jed drew a chart to organize his figures.

Jed made a chart to organize his figures. He wrote: *First I made a chart of all the events over the years by using multiplication & subtraction. The chart on page 16 represents what happened to the seeds over the years.*

Camilla recorded equations for each year. She wrote: *1st year—plants 2 × 2 = 4 − 1 = 3. 2nd year—plants 3 × 2 = 6 − 1 = 5.* She continued until she got to the tenth year where she calculated that Jack would get 1,026 seeds. Camilla finished her paper by writing: *The first number is how many seeds he planted. The 2nd number is how many seeds the sprouts produced. The last is how many seed all together.*

Judy also made a chart. In vertical columns, she wrote the number of years, seeds planted, seeds produced, and seeds eaten. To explain her chart, Judy wrote: *First I made a chart with 4 colomns and 10 rows. They are titled as you can see on pg. 1. Second I knew he had 2 seeds and ate none the first year. So, if he didn't eat any he planted 2 seeds. I wrote that in my chart. Third I multiplied on the side of my chart. I multiplied how many seeds he planted by 2. The 2 is there because you get two seeds from each plant. By doing that filled in my chart.* (Judy's chart appears on page 16.)

Deirdre made a bar graph to represent the number of seeds that grew each year. Along the bottom of her graph she wrote the number of years, 1 through 10. Along the side of her graph, she wrote the number of seeds in a vertical column. She only had room enough to number the seeds from 1 to 42, so she didn't have space to show how many seeds Jack received for the years 6 through 10. She wrote: *Well this graph shows the WIDE range between the years.*

"How did you go about making the graph?" I asked her.

"Well, at first I tried a graph that was very confusing," she said. "It had two parts to it and probably would have taken a million years to figure out what I was doing. Well, to help me with the results, I also used a calculator to receive the amounts of seeds each year. The graph really shows how much the seeds increase every year."

After about 45 minutes, I asked the students for their attention and explained the next part of the assignment. "When you're finished with the problem, look for patterns in the numbers you've written," I said. "Can someone give an example of a pattern you noticed?"

Federico said, "The number of years goes up by 1 every time. The years go 1, 2, 3, 4, 5, all the way to 10."

"That's one pattern," I confirmed. "Look for other patterns and describe them in words and numbers."

The class worked for another 20 minutes. I then asked volunteers to share their answers, explain how they solved the problem, and present the patterns they discovered.

"Jack always eats one seed, so there's a repeating pattern of 1, 1, 1, 1, 1, and so on," said Jonah. "There's another repeating pattern, kind of. The number of seeds is always doubling or being multiplied by 2."

Judy's chart showed by year how many seeds Jack started with, how many he ate, how many he planted, and the total number of seeds.

Facts to know
Planted 2 seeds the first year. He also didn't eat the first year.

The Magic Seeds

How many seeds did he get the tenth year? Answer 1,026

Years	How many seeds?	How many he ate?	How many he planted?	
1	2 seeds	0 seeds	2 seeds	2x2= 4
2	4 seeds	1 seed	3 seeds	3x2= 6
3	6 seeds	1 seed	5 seeds	5x2= 10
4	10 seeds	1 seed	9 seeds	9x2= 18
5	18 seeds	1 seed	17 seeds	17x2= 34
6	34 seeds	1 seed	33 seeds	33x2= 66
7	66 seeds	1 seed	65 seeds	65x2= 130
8	130 seeds	1 seed	129 seeds	129x2= 258
9	258 seeds	1 seed	257 seeds	257x2= 514
10	514 seeds	1 seed	513 seeds	513x2= 1,026

At the end of the 10th year he had

Patterns I saw
If you look in the colomn titled How many seeds? You will see the ones colomn match up.

2
4
6
10
18
34
66
130
258
514

@ The years grow by 1.
1
2
3
4
5
6
7
8
9
10

because you get two seeds filled in my chart.

My Steps

First I made a chart with 4 colomns and 10 rows. They are titled as you can see on pg.1.

Second I knew he had 2 seeds and ate none the first year. So, if he didn't eat any he planted 2 seeds. I wrote that in my chart.

Third I molliplied on the side of my chart. I multiplied how many seeds he planted by 2. The 2 is there from each plant. By doing that

I found the answer it how many seeds he had at the end of the 10th year and also in the same amount of seeds in the begining of the 11th year.

"I noticed that the number of seeds he plants, except for the first year, is always odd," said Paige. "And the number of plants he gets is always going to be an even number."

"Why do you think that happens?" I asked.

Paige paused a moment and then explained, "Because when he gets the seeds it's an even amount, and then he eats one seed so the number he plants will be odd."

"There's a pattern between the numbers of seeds he planted," said Jo. "He planted 2 seeds the first year and 3 the next year and the difference is 1. Then he planted 5 seeds, and the difference between 3 and 5 is 2. Then he planted 9 seeds, and the difference between 5 and 9 is 4. Then he planted 17 seeds, and the difference between 9 and 17 is 8. The difference keeps doubling."

"I saw a pattern in the numbers of seeds he got at the end of each year," said Wesley. "I put those numbers in a column, and there's a pattern with the numbers in the 1s place. These are the numbers: 2, 4, 6, 10, 18, 34, 66, 130, 258, 514, 1026. The pattern of the numbers in the 1s place starts with 4: 4, 6, 0, 8, 4, 6, 0, 8. It keeps going."

After the students had shared their ideas, I finished reading the story. I then said, "In the story, the author asks the reader to solve different problems than the one we solved today."

"Yeah, like when Jack gets married," said Cameron. "Jack and Alice both start eating a seed each year, so the problem changes."

"And when they have their wedding and they give seeds to their guests," added Deirdre. "The problem changes then, too."

"Does anyone have any questions about the problem we worked on today?" I asked.

"After the tenth year, Jack got 1,026 seeds," said Maggie. "I wonder if we could figure out how many seeds Jack would get after any year? Like after 50 or 100 years?"

"Does anyone have an idea how you might figure out how many seeds Jack would get after, say, 50 years?" I asked.

"We could keep doubling the numbers of seeds and subtracting 1 each time," suggested Camilla.

"We could use Wesley's pattern to help us," said Theo. "What was your pattern, Wesley?"

"That the answer will end in either 4, 6, zero, or 8," Wesley replied.

"Any other ideas?" I asked.

"The answer will be an even number," said Paige. "That's the pattern I noticed."

"We know it's going to be a huge number, if he got 1,026 seeds after only 10 years," said Larissa. "Doubling numbers makes things grow real fast."

Our discussion at the end of the lesson allowed the students to see how they could use the patterns they had found to solve larger problems. Patterns help children to see order, make sense of things, and predict what will happen. This problem challenged them to make use of patterns to predict and find an outcome.

Beasts of Burden

"Beasts of Burden" is a story from *The Man Who Counted: A Collection of Mathematical Adventures*, by Malba Tahan. In the story, the narrator and Beremiz, the wise mathematician, are traveling on a single camel when they encounter three fighting brothers. The brothers tell Beremiz that their father has left them 35 camels to divide three ways: $\frac{1}{2}$ to one brother, $\frac{1}{3}$ to another, and $\frac{1}{9}$ to the last. They can't figure out how to divide the inheritance. Beremiz suggests adding his camel to the 35, making 36, then explains that one brother would get 18 camels, one brother 12, and another 4. This computation leaves 2 camels left over: 1 to return to the narrator, and another, which Beremiz claims for himself. The story leads to an activity in which students work with division and fractions.

materials: color tiles 36 per group of 3-4 students

"Does anyone know what a beast of burden is?" Maryann Wickett asked her fifth and sixth graders.

"A horse or a donkey," Andie answered.

"Any other ideas?" she asked.

"A wild animal, I think," guessed Adriana.

"I brought a book today that I want to read to you," Maryann then said. "The book has many short stories in it, and one of them is called 'Beasts of Burden.' As I read the story, see if there are any clues that might help you understand what a beast of burden is."

Maryann's students listened with interest as she read the part where the three brothers argued and shouted about how to divide the 35 camels that they had inherited. Maryann read the sentence that explained that the oldest brother was to receive $\frac{1}{2}$ of the camels, the middle brother was to receive $\frac{1}{3}$, and the youngest, $\frac{1}{9}$. Maryann reviewed the information with the class.

"How many camels are there altogether?" she asked.

"Thirty-five," the class answered.

"How many camels is the oldest son supposed to get?" she asked.

"One-half!" they answered.

"What about the middle son?" she asked.

"One-third," they said.

"And the youngest?" she asked.

"One-ninth," they responded.

Maryann wrote on the board:

$$35\text{ camels}$$

Oldest	$\frac{1}{2}$
Middle	$\frac{1}{3}$
Youngest	$\frac{1}{9}$

"How many camels are half of 35?" she then inquired.

After a long pause, whispers broke out across the room as the students struggled with this problem. Finally, several hands shot up.

"That would be $17\frac{1}{2}$, I think," offered Monty. "But that's not a good answer because you can't have half a camel."

"Monty has a point," responded Maryann. "Talk in your groups and try to figure out some ways Beremiz can solve this problem."

A busy hum filled the classroom as the students began to share their ideas. After a few minutes, Maryann asked the students for their attention.

"How can Beremiz help the three brothers?" she asked.

"Beremiz could take 1 camel, and then there would be only 34, and 34 is an even number so it can be divided into halves equally," said Arleen.

"If there were some babies in the group, they could make two babies equal one adult," offered Shana.

"Maybe instead of splitting a camel, one brother could take a whole camel and the other brother who didn't get any could have the next baby camel that was born," said Edward.

"There's one clue or detail that I didn't tell you in the beginning that might give you some other ideas," Maryann said. "This story took place many years ago, before cars. People in Iraq used camels as their method of transportation. Beremiz and his friend were both riding on the friend's camel when they met up with the three arguing brothers."

"Oh, oh, I know!" shouted several students. Maryann called on Stu.

"If Beremiz added his friend's camel to the 35, that would make 36, and they could divide 36 into halves and thirds and ninths!" Stu exclaimed.

"That's exactly what Beremiz did," said Maryann. She then continued reading the story, stopping after the part where Beremiz says to the three brothers that he is going to divide the camels fairly.

"I'd like you to work together to come up with a possible solution that Beremiz might use to divide the camels," said Maryann. "You can work with your group and share ideas, but I want each of you to write your own solution. Remember, you can use words, numbers, and pictures to explain your reasoning."

As Maryann circulated throughout the room, she observed the students and listened to their conversations. Some students reached for their calculators, while others went to get counters.

One group of four seemed stuck, with no sign of leadership from any of its members. Maryann observed the students for a few minutes, then approached them to see if they had any idea about where to start.

"What was the question I asked you to think about?" she asked.

"We're supposed to figure out how the brothers divided the camels," Shana quickly responded.

"How many camels?" Maryann asked.

"They had 35," Denver said, "and Beremiz added his friend's, so that made 36."

"The oldest is supposed to get half, the middle a third, and the youngest a ninth," added Emilio.

"I'll get 36 counters, and we can divide them into halves, thirds, and ninths," said Shana, with an unsure voice.

"That makes sense," Denver said.

Feeling that the students understood the problem and had a way to begin, Maryann moved away from the group. Katrina, who was working in a different group, called Maryann over.

"Mrs. Wickett," she said, "I'm confused. We divided 36 by 2, and that made 18 camels for the oldest. Then we divided 36 into 3 groups and that made 12 for the middle brother. We divided 36 into 9 groups and that made 4 for the youngest. But when I added it all up, it only equaled 34 camels, and there were 36." Katrina had a perplexed look on her face.

"I know we did it right," interjected Barrett.

"Hmm, what did you expect them to add up to?" asked Maryann.

"Well, 36 because there are 36 camels," answered Chloe.

"Do your answers make sense?" asked Maryann.

"I think so," said Chloe. "I know we figured the amounts of camels the right way."

"I agree that your figuring was correct. Talk about what you think Beremiz would do in this situation," Maryann suggested. The students became involved in an animated discussion about what Beremiz might do.

After the students had had time to write their solutions, Maryann initiated a discussion. "What surprises did you run into while solving the problem?" she began.

"We expected the camels to equal 36 after we divided them among the brothers, but they equaled 34," Natasha reported.

"Raise your hand if your group ran into this problem," Maryann instructed. Most students raised their hands.

"What did you do about it?" asked Maryann.

"We checked our work on the calculator and then used counters," Lenora said. "When it came out the same the two different ways, we decided that Beremiz should get one of the extra ones for solving the problem and his friend should get his own camel back."

"We did something like that, too, but first we thought it was a trick question," offered Michaela.

"How many camels did each brother get after Beremiz added his friend's to the group?" Maryann asked.

"The oldest got 18, the middle one got 12, and the youngest got 4, and there were 2 extras," answered Sean. Maryann quickly noted this information on the board.

"Does this seem fair?" Maryann asked. "Were the wishes of the father honored?" The students were silent.

"When there were 35 camels, how many camels would the oldest have gotten?" Maryann then asked.

"Seventeen and a half," several students called out.

"What about the middle brother?" Maryann asked.

Several students quickly used calculators to find out, but most of them weren't sure how to make sense of 11.666666.

"The middle brother got 11 and a little more," announced Jagger.

"And the youngest brother?" asked Maryann.

"He'd get 3 and some more," stated Katrina.

"That could be really messy!" giggled Estevan.

Maryann added these numbers to what she had written on the board:

Oldest	*18*	*17½*
Middle	*12*	*11 and a little more*
Youngest	*4*	*3 and some more*

"Which way is better for the brothers?" Maryann asked.

"Well, they came out better with 36 camels, but I really don't get it," said Uma. "At the end, they lost 2 camels. Why did they get more when they still lost 2 camels?" she asked.

"Does anyone have an idea about that?" Maryann inquired.

"Maybe it has something to do with the extra parts," said Sean. None of the other students had anything to add.

Maryann then finished reading the story. Although the students were pleased to learn that Beremiz had solved the problem the same way most of them had suggested, they were still confused by the solution. Their confusion provided Maryann the opportunity to continue investigating the problem.

The Next Day

"Today I'd like to explore the problem of the camels a little further," said Maryann. She distributed a baggie of Color Tiles to each group. "Count out 36 for your group and return the rest to the baggie," Maryann directed. "Then use the tiles to show half of 36."

The students quickly counted out 36 tiles and divided them into two groups to show that ½ of 36 was 18. Maryann called on Chloe to explain her group's answer.

"It's 18," she said, "because we made two lines and they're the same. They each have 18."

Jagger explained how his group did it. "We took 2 at a time and put them in different piles," he said. "Each pile has 18."

"I'd like each of you to record the answer to ½ of 36," Maryann said, "and explain how you got it. You can use words and pictures along with the numbers. Then do the same to figure ⅓ of 36, and then do ⅑ of 36."

As the students worked, Maryann circulated throughout the room. After the students had had time to record, she called the class back to order, asked the students to report the answers, and recorded on the board:

$$\tfrac{1}{2} \text{ of } 36 = 18$$
$$\tfrac{1}{3} \text{ of } 36 = 12$$
$$\tfrac{1}{9} \text{ of } 36 = 4$$

"If we add up the number of camels each brother got—18 plus 12 plus 4—we find out how many camels they got altogether," Maryann said.

"It's 34," Denver said. "What happened to the 2 extra camels?"

"Let me try to help you understand," Maryann said. "First, let me ask you about representing the fractions differently." She wrote on the board:

$$\tfrac{1}{2} = {}^{18}\!/_{36}$$
$$\tfrac{1}{3} = {}^{12}\!/_{36}$$
$$\tfrac{1}{9} = {}^{4}\!/_{36}$$

"Who can explain why these sentences make sense?" Maryann asked. "Talk in your groups for a moment, and then I'll have volunteers explain."

Stu explained why $\tfrac{1}{2}$ and ${}^{18}\!/_{36}$ are equivalent. "If you add 18 and another 18, you get 36, and that means that 18 is half of 36, so ${}^{18}\!/_{36}$ is just the same as $\tfrac{1}{2}$."

Michaela added, "It's just different numbers, but they mean the same because 2 is 2 times 1 and 36 is 2 times 18."

Max used division to figure out the fractional parts of 36.

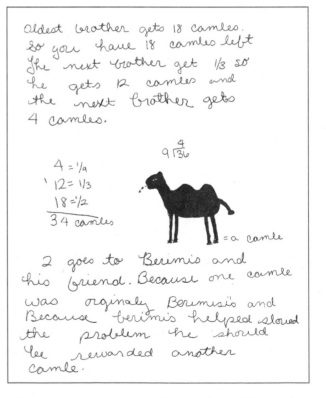

After solving the problem, Elise drew a spitting camel.

"What about the other two sentences?" Maryann asked.

Monty said, "It's like Michaela said. For $\frac{1}{3}$, 1 times 3 is 3, and 12 times 3 is 36. It works for the other because 1 times 4 is 4, and 9 times 4 is 36." To help others understand, Maryann pointed to the fractions as he explained.

Katrina said, "When we figured out how much was $\frac{1}{3}$ of 36, we divided the tiles into three groups, and there were 12 in each, so that makes $\frac{12}{36}$. We did $\frac{1}{9}$ the same way."

Riley added, "The numbers get bigger, but the amounts don't."

Although these students gave their explanations confidently, Maryann wasn't sure that everyone in the class understood why the fractions were equivalent. However, she continued, "If we add up the three fractions—$\frac{18}{36}$, $\frac{12}{36}$, and $\frac{4}{36}$ — we get $\frac{34}{36}$." Maryann wrote on the board:

$$\frac{18}{36} + \frac{12}{36} + \frac{4}{36} = \frac{34}{36}$$

"Ooooh," Max said, "that's why there are 2 extras."

"Yeah, there are 2 left over," Estevan added.

"If 2 are left over, what does that tell you about this set of three fractions?" questioned Maryann.

"It doesn't equal the whole group," Monty said. "The 2 extras means that there are leftovers, so the fractions probably don't equal up to 1."

"I agree with Monty," said Arleen. "Because not all the camels were used, so the parts don't make the whole."

"What fraction would they have to add up to in order to make the whole?" Maryann asked.

Arleen, Monty, and Chloe answered in unison: "$\frac{36}{36}$!" They giggled.

"I agree that $\frac{18}{36}$, $\frac{12}{36}$, and $\frac{4}{36}$ do not add up to one whole," Maryann confirmed. "And because these fractions are just different names for $\frac{1}{2}$, $\frac{1}{3}$, and $\frac{1}{9}$, then those fractions don't add up to one whole, either." Maryann wrote on the board:

$$\frac{1}{2} + \frac{1}{3} + \frac{1}{9} = \textit{less than one whole } (\tfrac{34}{36})$$

"Why didn't the father just tell the sons how many camels they would each get?" Edward asked. "Then there wouldn't be a problem."

"I know," Katrina said. "He didn't know how many camels there would be. I mean, some could have had babies or something. Then they'd still fight."

"Why do you think the father chose those particular fractions?" Maryann asked. "Do you think the father wanted to cause his children to quarrel? Do you think he realized the fractions he chose did not equal 1? Why do you think he chose the fractions he did?"

"I don't think he wanted his sons to fight, so I think he didn't know the fractions wouldn't work out right and use up all the camels," explained Uma. "Maybe he didn't know how to do math and wanted better things for his sons."

"Maybe he wanted his sons to cooperate with each other," said Celeste.

"Maybe the father never learned to divide evenly," added Natasha.

"What fractions could the father have chosen to use up all 36 camels?" Maryann asked.

"Well, $\frac{1}{3}$ plus $\frac{1}{3}$ plus $\frac{1}{3}$ equals 1, and that would make 12, 12, and 12 for each brother, which is 36," said Jerry. Maryann recorded on the board:

$$\frac{1}{3} + \frac{1}{3} + \frac{1}{3} = 1$$

"One son could get $\frac{1}{2}$ which is 18, one son could get $\frac{1}{3}$ which is 12, and the last son could get $\frac{6}{36}$, and that equals 1 because there are no leftovers," Stu explained. Maryann recorded:

$$\frac{1}{2} + \frac{1}{3} + \frac{6}{36} = 1$$

"I have another way to write what Stu suggested," Maryann said. She wrote:

$$\frac{1}{2} + \frac{1}{3} + \frac{1}{6} = 1$$

"Raise your hand if this makes sense to you," Maryann said. She waited until about eight students had raised their hands. She called on Natasha to explain.

"It's like we did before," she said. "It works because in $\frac{1}{6}$, 6 is 6 times as big as 1, and in $\frac{6}{36}$ it's the same — 36 is 6 times as much as 6."

"Would $\frac{34}{36}$, $\frac{1}{36}$, and $\frac{1}{36}$ work?" Maryann asked the class.

"That would work and so would $\frac{32}{36}$, $\frac{2}{36}$, $\frac{2}{36}$ because 32 plus 2 plus 2 equals 36 and $\frac{36}{36}$ makes a whole," offered Uma.

Maryann completed the sentence she began and added what Uma suggested. The list now contained the following:

$$\frac{1}{3} + \frac{1}{3} + \frac{1}{3} = 1$$
$$\frac{1}{2} + \frac{1}{3} + \frac{6}{36} = 1$$
$$\frac{1}{2} + \frac{1}{3} + \frac{1}{6} = 1$$
$$\frac{34}{36} + \frac{1}{36} + \frac{1}{36} = 1$$
$$\frac{32}{36} + \frac{2}{36} + \frac{2}{36} = 1$$

Students continued to suggest other sets of three fractions with denominators of 36 that added to 1, and Maryann recorded them. After recording about 10 sentences, she posed a question.

"How many more sets of three fractions that add up to 1 do you think there are?" she asked.

"I think there are an infinite number of ways . . . and that's a lot!" Emilio announced.

Maryann asked the students to work in their groups to figure out and record additional sets of three fractions that would use all 36 camels. After 10 minutes, Maryann interrupted the students and had groups report their findings. All of the groups had used fractions with denominators of 36.

"Take a moment and think about the father's wishes for his sons," Maryann said. "Examine the sets of fractions on the board and decide which set of fractions he might have chosen that would have used up all 36 camels." After giving the students a few moments to think, Maryann called on Arleen.

"I think $\frac{20}{36}$, $\frac{10}{36}$, and $\frac{6}{36}$ because he wanted $\frac{1}{2}$ for the oldest and 20 is just a little more than a half," offered Arleen. "He wanted $\frac{1}{3}$ for the middle and $\frac{1}{9}$ for the youngest, and those are close, too."

Noel estimated what the father might have given to his sons so that all 36 camels would be used.

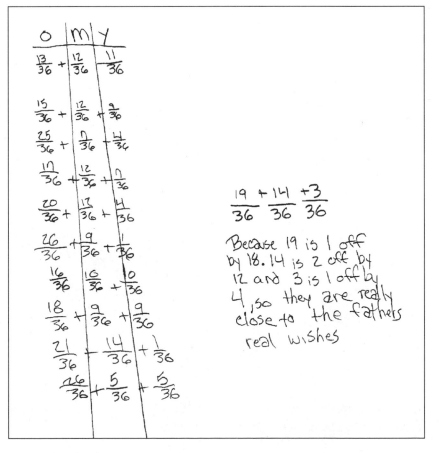

Andie chose ¹⁹/₃₆, ¹⁴/₃₆, and ³/₃₆ because the numerators were close to the numbers of camels given to each son.

$$\frac{19}{36} + \frac{14}{36} + \frac{3}{36}$$

Because 19 is 1 off by 18. 14 is 2 off by 12 and 3 is 1 off by 4, so they are really close to the father's real wishes

"I kind of agree with Arleen," Noel said. "I just gave the oldest one 2 extra, so I think $^{20}/_{36}$, $^{12}/_{36}$, and $^4/_{36}$. I think this is close to the real thing."

"I think that $^{19}/_{36}$, $^{14}/_{36}$, and $^3/_{36}$ are closer to 18, 12, and 4, which are the numbers they got," Andie explained.

Because the students had relied only on fractions with denominators of 36, Maryann suspected that they didn't fully grasp that $^1/_2 + ^1/_3 + ^1/_9$ was the same as $^{18}/_{36} + ^{12}/_{36} + ^4/_{36}$ and also didn't total 1. She felt this lack of understanding probably occurred because of their limited experience with situations involving fractions with unlike denominators. She decided to change the focus by asking the students to explore sets of three fractions that would account for all the camels when there were different numbers of camels to divide.

"I'm curious about fractions that you could use for numbers of camels other than 36," Maryann said to the class. "You've found many sets of three fractions that use all 36 camels. What if there were only 3 camels? Is there a set of three fractions that would divide 3 camels so there weren't any extras? Or what about for any other number of camels?"

"I think you can do it for 3, but I don't think you can do it for 1 or 2 because that would be parts of camels," explained Max.

"I think you can do $^1/_3$ and $^1/_3$ and $^1/_3$ for 3, and that you could use those fractions for 6, but I'm not sure," said Emilio, cautiously.

"How could you test your idea?" Maryann asked.

"I could use tiles," Emilio answered. "I could use six tiles and divide them into three groups. Oh, yeah, it would work; there would be two in each group."

Maryann then gave directions. "I'd like each of you to investigate possible fractions for different numbers of camels," she said. "Suppose the father wanted to be sure there wouldn't be any quarrels or leftover camels, and because he wasn't sure how many camels he'd have when he died, he decided to investigate what fractions would work for different numbers." Maryann pointed to a large chart she had prepared with the numbers from 1 to 48 listed vertically down the left side.

"Let's investigate the numbers on this chart," she continued. "Choose a number to explore, and write your initials beside it. Then investigate sets of three fractions that would divide that number of camels with no extras. When you've found at least three sets of three fractions, record them on the chart next to your number. Then we'll examine the chart and see what we can discover."

The students chose their numbers and began working. Maryann left the chart up, and the students investigated their numbers throughout the day.

The Third Day

As the students began the third day of this investigation, Maryann still had a nagging doubt about their understanding of combining fractions with unlike denominators. When recording sets of fractions on the chart, the students wrote only fractions whose denominators were the same as the number they were investigating.

Maryann quickly wrote on the board the following information:

½ of 36 camels = 18
⅓ of 36 camels = 12
⅑ of 36 camels = 4
This uses up 34 camels in all.

"What does this information tell you about the fractions ½, ⅓, and ⅑?" Maryann asked the class. They had talked about this several times before, but Maryann knows that giving students a chance to think about the same idea several times can help them cement their understanding.

"I think that they don't use all the camels, so the fractions don't equal a whole," Edward replied. Some students still looked a little puzzled.

"What if the father had left 18 camels?" Maryann asked. "Would these fractions use up all of the 18 camels? Or would there be leftovers?" About half the class thought there would be leftovers and half thought all the camels would be used.

Sean explained his reasoning. "I think there would be leftovers because there were leftovers with 36, and 18 is half of 36, and so I think if you are using the same fractions there would be half the leftovers," he said.

"What happens with 18?" Maryann said. "Take 18 tiles for the camels and figure out how much each son would get if the oldest got ½, the middle one got ⅓, and the youngest got ⅑. Record what you discover on your paper."

The students took only a few moments to discover that there would be 1 leftover camel. Maryann recorded their findings on the board:

	36			18	
½ =		18	½ =		9
⅓ =		12	⅓ =		6
⅑ =		4	⅑ =		2
Total:		34	*Total:*		17
Leftovers:		2	*Leftovers:*		1

"I see a pattern," said Michaela. Maryann asked her to explain.

"I notice that everything is half . . . or double, depending on which way you go, like 9 is half of 18 or two 9s make 18," said Michaela.

"I bet that you'll ask us to try 9 . . . or maybe 72," Laurie speculated.

"Let's see what happens with 9," said Maryann. Again, the students quickly tried this, recording the results on their papers.

"What did you find out?" Maryann asked when the students finished.

"My prediction about 9 being half of 18 was right, and there was a leftover of a half," said Kennon. As Kennon reported, Maryann recorded:

	36			18			9	
½ =		18	½ =		9	½ =		4½
⅓ =		12	⅓ =		6	⅓ =		3
⅑ =		4	⅑ =		2	⅑ =		1
Total:		34	*Total:*		17	*Total:*		8½
Leftovers:		2	*Leftovers:*		1	*Leftovers:*		½

"So what's happening here?" asked Maryann.

"The fractions don't add up to a whole, so they can't use up all of a number," Lydia responded.

"If the father wanted to give his oldest son $\frac{1}{2}$ of the camels and his middle son $\frac{1}{3}$ of the camels, what fraction would he have to give his youngest son to use up all 36 camels? Figure out what the fraction is and explain your reasoning on your paper," Maryann told the class.

As Maryann walked around the room listening and talking with the students, her uneasiness about their understanding began to ease. Most students quickly saw that the fraction for the youngest son would have to be $\frac{6}{36}$, and they saw that it was the same as $\frac{1}{6}$.

"Let's look at the sets of three fractions you recorded on the chart," said Maryann. "What do you notice?"

"No one picked 1 or 2 because that wasn't enough camels to divide among the three brothers," Max observed. "It looks like we can't use them because there's not enough to go around."

"It seems as if the bigger the number gets, the more fractions there are, like there are more ways to make 48 than 18," added Andie.

"I notice you could make nine combinations with three numbers in the numerators if the lower numbers stay the same, just by switching the order of what each brother gets," Arleen shared.

"What do you notice about the numerators?" Maryann asked.

"They're mostly even numbers," said Roger.

"All the numerators were lower than the denominators and the three numerators added up to the denominators," added Edward.

Maryann posed a new question for the students.

"You saw that it's possible to use $\frac{1}{2}$, $\frac{1}{3}$, and $\frac{1}{6}$ to divide up 36 camels," she said, and added those fractions to the chart next to the 36. "Could you use these fractions for any other number on the chart?"

The students were excited about this question, and they began to make predictions and test their ideas.

"I guessed 72 because it's two 36s. I tried it and it worked!" said Elise.

"Mrs. Wickett, Kennon thinks 9 billion will work!" said Chloe, giggling.

"Ask him to explain his thinking to you," Maryann responded.

"I know that 9 billion is a multiple of all three numbers and so I'm sort of sure it would work, but I don't have the tiles to prove it!" Kennon explained.

After a few minutes, Maryann asked the students for their attention.

"Let's record all of the possible numbers that you've found," Maryann said.

"72 works—$\frac{1}{2}$ is 36, $\frac{1}{3}$ is 24, and $\frac{1}{6}$ is 12," reported Elise. "It's just like 36, except that everything is doubled."

"I think 48 works: $\frac{1}{2}$ is 24, $\frac{1}{3}$ is 16, and $\frac{1}{6}$ is 8," explained Celeste.

"And 30 works, too," said Monty, " because $\frac{1}{2}$ is 15, $\frac{1}{3}$ is 10, and $\frac{1}{6}$ is 5. Add it up and, like magic, it equals 30!"

Maryann recorded her students' findings in a chart to encourage them to look for patterns:

Number:	72	48	30	60	6	12	96	9,000,000,000
$\frac{1}{2}$:	36	24	15	30	3	6	48	4,500,000,000
$\frac{1}{3}$:	24	16	10	20	2	4	32	3,000,000,000
$\frac{1}{6}$:	12	8	5	10	1	2	16	1,500,000,000

"Oh! I see a pattern!" Andie exclaimed. "All the numbers that are possible are even numbers and all are multiples of 6 . . . so I bet that any number that is a product of 6 will work!"

"I wonder why it works with 6?" asked Kennon. "I wonder if there are any numbers that aren't multiples of 6 that would be possible with $\frac{1}{2}$, $\frac{1}{3}$, and $\frac{1}{6}$?"

"I wonder if any odd numbers are multiples of 6?" added Uma.

"I wonder how you would find out other fractions that equaled one whole and their possible numbers?" Edward asked.

"I am hearing all kinds of interesting, wonderful questions that you're asking as a result of this investigation," Maryann observed. "Please write on your paper at least one idea you are wondering about."

The students completed this three-day lesson by writing down their "I wonder" questions. These questions can be used to spark new investigations involving fractions.

Note: A similar problem can be found in *Stories to Solve: Folk Tales from Around the World*, by George Shannon. In the story called, "Dividing the Horses," $\frac{1}{2}$ of 17 horses has to be given to one son, $\frac{1}{3}$ to another son, and $\frac{1}{9}$ to the third son.

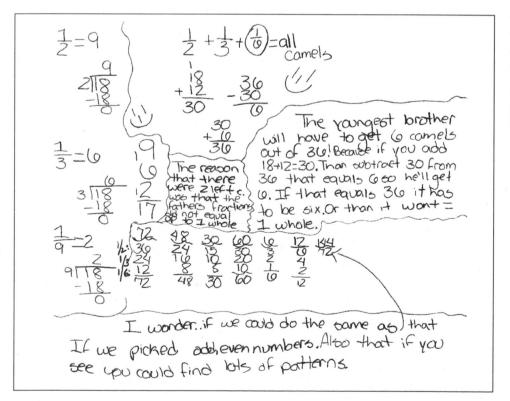

When Lenora found that 72, 48, 30, 60, 6, and 12 could be divided equally by $\frac{1}{2}$, $\frac{1}{3}$, and $\frac{1}{6}$, she wondered what patterns she could find.

Counting on Frank

In *Counting on Frank*, by Rod Clement, a precocious boy makes endless calculations. He figures that the average ball-point pen can draw a line 7,000 feet long before running out of ink, that 24 Franks (Frank is his dog) can fit into his bedroom, that it would take 11 hours and 45 minutes to fill the entire bathroom with water, and much more. Witty comments and graphic illustrations accompany each unusual measurement calculation. The boy's statement that if he grew at the rate of the tree in his yard, he'd be almost 50 feet tall suggests several problems for students to solve that challenge them to reason proportionally.

When I held up the cover of *Counting on Frank*, many of Carole Smith's fourth and fifth graders immediately recognized the funny-looking boy with the spiked hair and his pet dog, Frank. Some students said that they had heard the story before.

"It's a neat book!" exclaimed Anne-Marie.

"I remember all of those peas," Cameron chimed in.

"It seems as if many of you are familiar with the story," I said.

"We could listen to it again," Jed said.

"Yes!" others chorused.

I started reading the book and stopped on the second page to show the students the picture of the boy surrounded by 24 Franks in his bedroom. "The boy in the story figures that 24 Franks could fit in his bedroom," I said. "How many Franks do you think could fit in the classroom?"

"Are the dogs piled on top of one another?" asked Maggie.

"Although it looks as if they are in the picture, let's say we'd just fill up the floor with Franks," I answered. "Talk about this at your table and come up with an estimate."

After a minute or two, several hands went up, and I asked for the students' attention. I called on Arturo.

"I think there could be about 100 Franks in the room," he said, "because on the other page, Frank is sitting next to his owner and it looks like he's about 3 feet long. So I imagined dogs that big in the room, and it seems like there would be about 100."

Tano had a different estimate. "I think there could be about 260 Franks in our room because the dog looks small and dogs could snuggle up to one another," he said.

"I estimate 150 because I think we're about twice as long as Frank, and 30 of us fit easily in the room," explained Calie.

"Calie, if we're about twice as long as Frank, and 30 of us fit in the room, what does that tell you about how many Franks fit in the room?" I asked.

"Hmmm," Calie responded. "Well, twice 30 is 60, so maybe a little more than 60 Franks could fill up the room."

I then continued reading the story. The students laughed when the boy's mother says that his dad's feet smell. They loved the picture of the boy and his family, waist deep in green peas, eating dinner. Their favorite part was the picture of the house-sized toaster shooting giant pieces of toast into the air, endangering low-flying aircraft.

When I finished reading the story, I turned back to the part where the boy and Frank are standing next to a tree. The illustration shows the boy's giant feet next to a very small Frank. "I'm going to read this page to you again, and then I have a mathematical question for you to think about," I told the class. I read, "We've got a tree in our yard. It grows about 6 feet every year. If I had grown at the same speed, I'd now be almost 50 feet tall!"

I then said, "The boy says that he would be almost 50 feet tall if he had grown 6 feet every year. My question is: How old is the boy? Talk about this with your group. When you've figured it out, explain with numbers and in writing how you solved it. You may work together, but you should each record your own solution."

I paused and looked around the room. "Are there any questions?" I asked.

"Do we figure out exactly how old the boy is or about how old he is?" Larissa asked.

"I'm going to leave that decision up to you," I said.

No other students had questions, so they all got to work. After spending a few minutes talking in their groups, most students began writing. Calculators were readily available; some students chose to use them and others didn't.

The students solved the problem in a variety of ways. Some added 6s in their heads until they got close to 50. Some thought about what number they could multiply by 6 to get to 50. Some divided 50 by 6. Some students organized information into a chart to figure out the answer. Some students used a calculator and divided 50 by 6, ending up with 8.3333333 as an answer. While some didn't know what to do with the decimal point followed by the 3s, most of the students knew that 0.3333333 meant about a third. Some students translated a third of a year into months.

Jansen's first answer didn't make sense. He wrote: *I think he would be 33 years old because I ÷ 50 ÷ 6 and I got 8.3333333 and I covered up the 8 and the 5 3ths and I got 33, so I think he would be 33. and other thing how I got 33 is I added 25 + 8 and I got 33. and an other way how I got the answer is I added 23 + 10 and that equaled 33.*

It seemed that the ways Jansen reported to make 33 had nothing to do with the problem I'd posed. After listening to him read his paper, I asked questions to refocus him on the problem and nudge him to rely on reason and common sense.

"What's the mathematical question you're trying to solve?" I asked.

Jansen sat quietly for a moment, thinking. Finally, he said tentatively, "We're trying to find out how old the boy is?"

"That's right," I responded. "You said the boy is 33 years old. Do you think the boy in the story is 33? Does he look 33?"

"Not really," Jansen replied.

"How old does he look to you?" I asked.

"He looks like he's my age or maybe a little younger," he said.

"What information do you know from the book that could help you find out how old he is?" I asked.

"Well, I know that he grew 6 feet each year," Jansen responded. "The boy said that if he grew like the tree, he would be almost 50 feet tall. So I divided 6 into 50."

"When you divided those numbers on the calculator, you got 8.3333333. That number means 8 and a little more. It's a number that's more than 8 and less than 9; it's in-between," I explained.

Jo's paper shows the several false starts she made before deciding that the boy was between 8 and 9 years old.

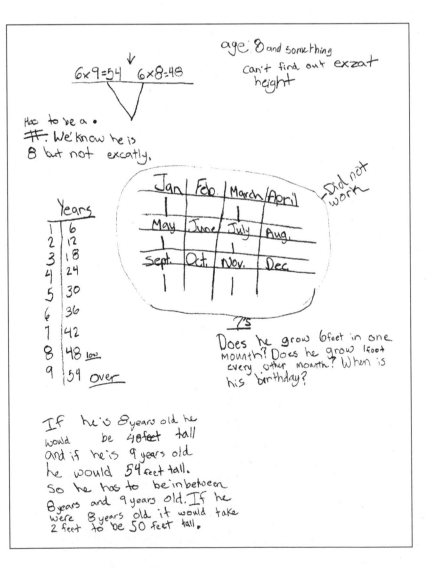

"Hey! Maybe he's around 8 years old! That makes sense!" Jansen exclaimed.

Paige also used a calculator. She interpreted the answer in terms of months and wrote: *What we did was divided 50 ÷ 6 = the answer we came up to was 8.3333333. We think he is 8 and 4 months years old. ⅓ of a year.*

Camilla, who was working with Paige, explained why 8.3333333 meant the same as 8 years and 4 months. She wrote: *We think he is 8 and 4 months. ⅓ of a year 12 ÷ 3 = 4 months.*

Jo solved the problem without a calculator. She made a chart and recorded how tall the boy would be each year. She recorded that the first year he would be 6 feet, the second year 12 feet, and so on. When she got to eight years old, Jo found that the boy would be 48 feet tall. For his ninth year, she recorded that he would be 54 feet tall. Jo wrote low next to the 48 and over next to the 54.

"He has to be in between 8 and 9 years old," Jo told me. "He needs 2 more feet to be 50 feet. When he's 8, he would be 48 feet tall."

Jo had also recorded some questions she was wondering about: *Does he grow 6 feet in one mounth? Does he grow 1 foot every other mounth? When is his birthday?*

Jed used proportional reasoning to find a solution. He wrote: *The way I figured this problem out is we took our multipication charts and found that the closest number we could get to 50 using multipication was 48. We figured out that there there are 12 months in a year and if he grows 1 foot every 2 months he would grow to be 48 feet in 8 years. But, there was still 2 feet leftover so if you used these facts you would end up with 4 months and 8 years.*

Jed's paper shows how he reasoned proportionally to find a solution.

Ephraim also used multiplication. He started with *6 × 1 = 6* feet for the first year. Then he continued with *6 × 2 = 12, 6 × 3 = 18, 6 × 4 = 24, 6 × 5 = 30, 6 × 6 = 36, 6 × 7 = 42, 6 × 8 = 48.* "I got up to 48 because it's close to 50," he told me. "I came up with 8 years."

In a class discussion, several students volunteered to share their work with the class. Everyone agreed that the boy was somewhere between 8 and 9 years old.

"Now that you've had the experience of figuring out how old the boy is, I have a new mathematical question for you," I said. "I'm 40 years old now. If I had grown 6 feet each year since I was born, how tall would I be now? Talk to the person next to you and see what you come up with figuring mentally." The students were excited about this question, and their discussions were animated.

After a few minutes, I interrupted the class. "How tall do you think I would be?" I asked.

"I think you would be 240 feet tall," Flint said. "I know this because I multiplied 40 by 6 and it came to 240. It's kind of like the first problem we did. I solved it like Ephraim explained." Other students nodded their agreement.

I posed another problem. "Figure out how tall you'd be now if you had grown 6 feet each year since you were born," I instructed. "This time, record your solution and explain your thinking using numbers and words."

As I walked around the room, I overheard Judy say, "Doing the first problem really helps us solve this one!"

Anne-Marie used a chart to organize her work. She wrote the years in one vertical column and on the other side of the table she recorded her height for each year. She wrote: *I am 10 years old. I know I would be 60 feet tall and two months because I did this chart. and each year I grew 6 feet a year and I added 6 feet a year. So My tottol was 60 feet and two months*

Anne-Marie made a chart to show how she knew she would be 60 feet tall.

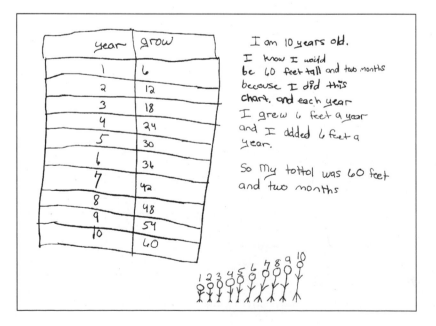

Aubrey was interested in figuring precisely. He wrote: *I am exactly 64 feet because when 2 months = 1 foot 1 year is 6 feet, that is 60 feet in 10 years. So that means 8 months is 4 feet, so that must mean that I am 64 feet.*

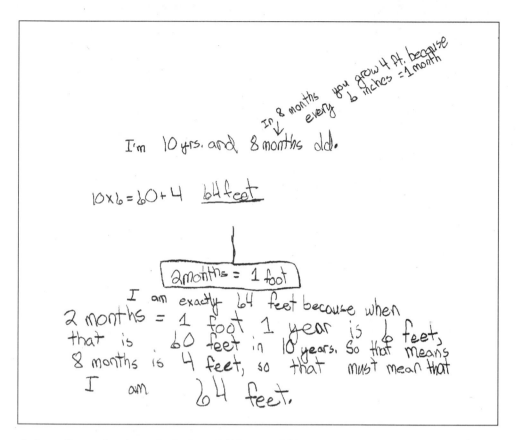

Aubrey figured out precisely how tall he would be.

Jo was also concerned with being precise, and she figured out exactly how tall she would be to the month. She wrote: *I am 10 years old and I grow 6 feet every year so 10 × 6 = 60. You grow 6 inch. every mounth and it has been 8 mounths since my last birthday, so 6 × 8 = 48. 48 ÷ 12 = 4 feet. You ÷ 12 because 12 inch. in one foot. 4 feet + 60 feet = 64 feet.*

Judy decided to have fun with the fact that she was born in a leap year. She wrote: *I'm born on leap day so my birthday only comes once every four years but I have been alive 10 years a [and] 8 months. My birthdate: Feb. 29, 1984. Each year I grow 6 in. Leap year age: 2, 2 year, 8 months, 32 months leap year.*

"How tall would you be if you counted all of the years and months?" I asked her.

"My actual age is 10 years and 8 months," she said. She referred to her paper and explained, "That's 128 months because 10 times 12 equals 120, plus 8 months is 128 months. 128 times 6 inches each month is 768 inches. And 768 inches divided by 12 is 64 feet tall."

Dylan added 6 ten times to get 60 feet. He told me, "I'm turning 10 this month so I added an extra 6 feet."

Maggie worked with fractions to solve the problem. "I'm 10 years old and 7 months," she said. "I multiplied 10 times 6 feet and got 60 feet. Then I multiplied 6 inches by 7 months and got 42 inches. Then I divided 42 into 12 inches and got 3 and a half feet. I added that to 60 and got 63½ feet tall! That's tall!!"

When the students finished sharing their papers, Deirdre raised her hand. "If we really had grown 6 feet every year, I wonder who the tallest person would be and who the shortest would be?" she asked.

"Does anyone have an idea?" I asked.

"The tallest person would be the oldest!" exclaimed Wesley.

"And the shortest person?" I asked.

"The youngest!" everyone answered.

"I know who the tallest person would be. It would be you," said Calie, laughing.

"Here's your assignment for tomorrow," I told them. "You all know how tall you would be if you grew at a rate of 6 feet a year. I want you to find out what you would be as tall as. In other words, with what would you be able to see eye to eye?" As I was leaving, I heard Cameron ask a friend, "What in the world is 66 feet tall?"

Each Orange Had 8 Slices: A Counting Book

In *Each Orange Had 8 Slices: A Counting Book*, by Paul Giganti, Jr., each two-page spread shows people, animals, or objects grouped in three ways, then asks questions that require the reader to find the total number of each object in the picture. For example, the author writes, "I saw 4 trees. Each tree had 3 bird's nests. Each bird's nest had 2 spotted eggs." He then asks, "How many trees were there? How many bird's nests were there? How many spotted eggs were there in all?" The lesson based on this book gives children an opportunity to practice mental multiplication and combine story writing with mathematics.

materials: none

When I read *Each Orange Had 8 Slices* to John Swaim's fourth graders, they were in the middle of a unit on multiplication. Before reading the book, I explained to the students that they would write their own mathematical problems after I finished reading the book.

"As I read, pay attention to the problems that the author poses on each page," I said, "and think about how you would solve them."

After I read the first five pages, the students were eager to share their thoughts. Hands were waving in the air, and I could hear those familiar sounds that students make when they are dying to say something. I stopped reading to allow them to share their ideas.

"Who would like to tell us what kinds of things you've noticed about the book so far?" I asked.

"It's about math," Dawn said.

"You need to use times," Vivian observed.

"You're not supposed to say times," Anson said. "You're supposed to say *multiplication*."

"Would you agree with Vivian that you could use multiplication to solve the problems?" I asked, emphasizing the word *multiplication*. The students nodded in agreement.

"What else do you notice about the book?" I asked.

"You have to multiply three times when you solve a problem," Sheila said.

"Sheila, would you give us an example?" I asked.

"Could you turn to the page with the tricycles?" she asked.

I quickly turned back to the pages with three children riding tricycles and held it up for the class to see.

"See, there are three children and each one is riding one tricycle and each tricycle has three wheels," said Sheila. "The author asks how many kids, how many tricycles, then how many wheels in all. You could get the answer by going 3 times 1 times 3. You use three numbers when you multiply."

I continued reading the story, stopping on the spread that shows four trees, three bird's nests in each tree, and two spotted eggs in each nest.

"How many trees are there?" I asked.

"Four," answered the class.

"How many bird's nests are there?" I asked.

"Twelve," they responded.

"How many spotted eggs are there in all?" I continued. "Raise your hand when you get the answer." After a few moments, several hands shot up.

"There are 24 spotted eggs," said Colin.

"How do you know that?" I asked.

"Because 4 trees multiplied by 3 bird's nests is 12. Then 12 nests multiplied by 2 spotted eggs is 24," he explained.

When I got to the last page of the book, I read the poem:

"As I was going to St. Ives,
I met a man with 7 wives.
Every wife had 7 sacks.
Every sack had 7 cats.
Every cat had 7 kittens.
Kittens, cats, sacks, and wives,
How many were going to St. Ives?"

The class was stunned. "Does anyone have an idea?" I asked. No one raised a hand.

"I'm going to read the last page again, and I want you to listen carefully to what the author says," I said. This time, I wrote the poem on the board and had the students read along with me. Then I asked them to discuss the problem with the people at their table. After a minute or two, several hands were waving in the air. I asked the students for their attention, and I called on Malcolm.

"I think there were 2,401 things going to St. Ives," he said. "I multiplied 7 times 7 times 7 times 7 and got 2,401."

"Does anyone else have an idea to share?" I asked.

"It's a trick," Vivian giggled. "The author is asking how many were going to St. Ives, not how many altogether. Only one person was going to St. Ives."

Vivian's revelation received a collective groan from the class. Then the students started to laugh at the clever problem that had stumped them.

"The author asked a different question at the end of this problem," I said. "What are the questions that he asks at the end of the other problems in the book?"

"With the tricycles, he asked how many kids first. Then he asked how many tricycles. Then how many wheels in all," explained Cindy.

"So, as Sheila said earlier, there are three questions the author asks," I said. "The big question at the end asks about the total number of the last thing, like the wheels."

I walked to the board and made a chart with five columns. Then I handed the book to Annelise and asked her to read aloud her favorite page.

She read: "On my way to the zoo I saw 3 waddling ducks." In the first column, I wrote:

3 waddling ducks

Annelise continued reading: "Each duck had 4 baby ducks trailing behind." In the second column, I wrote:

4 baby ducks

Annelise then read: "Each duck said, 'QUACK, QUACK, QUACK.'" In the third column, I wrote:

Quack, Quack, Quack

In column four, I wrote the three questions:

How many waddling ducks were there?
How many baby ducks were there?
How many quacks were there in all?

"In column five, I want to write the multiplication sentence that tells about the story," I told them.

"It's 3 times 4 times 3, and that equals 36," offered Anastasia. I recorded Anastasia's idea in column five:

$3 \times 4 \times 3 = 36$

"If you were the author of your own story, what things would you include?" I asked. I called on Trudy.

"My story would go like this," she began. "I was on my way trick-or-treating, and I saw three pumpkins." I recorded *3 pumpkins* in the first column.

"Each pumpkin had one face, and each face had 10 teeth," she continued. I recorded *1 face* in column two and *10 teeth* in column three.

"What three questions should I write in column four?" I asked her.

"How many pumpkins? How many faces? How many teeth in all?" answered Trudy.

"And the multiplication sentence?" I asked.

"It's 3 times 1 times 10 equals 30 teeth," she responded as I recorded.

"What other things could we include in our stories?" I asked.

"We could put 10 trees, 8 branches on each tree, and 5 twigs on each branch. That would be 10 times 8 times 5," Billy suggested.

"How could we solve that problem?" I asked.

"I know," said Billy, "10 times 8 equals 80 and 80 times 5 is, hmmm." He was stuck.

"Can anyone think of a way we could multiply 80 times 5?" I asked.

"Well, 100 times 5 is 500," said Sheila. "And 80 is 20 less than 100 and 20 times 5 is 100. So 500 minus 100 equals 400. The answer is 400."

"How about another way?" I probed.

"Well, 8 times 5 is 40, so you just add a zero to 40 and you get 400," offered Glen.

"Is there another way we could multiply 80 times 5?" I asked.

"You could write 80 down on your paper," explained Vivian.

"Let me record what you say on the board," I said.

"Okay, then write 5 below the zero in 80 and make a multiplication sign," continued Vivian. "Then you multiply zero times 5, which is zero, and put the zero down. Then you multiply 8 times 5 equals 40. You put the 40 in front of the zero and you have 400."

"Now I want each of you to write your own story," I told the class. "Remember that you need to include an illustration to go along with your story. Are there any questions?"

"Can we do more than one story?" asked Cindy.

"Yes, after your first story is complete," I replied.

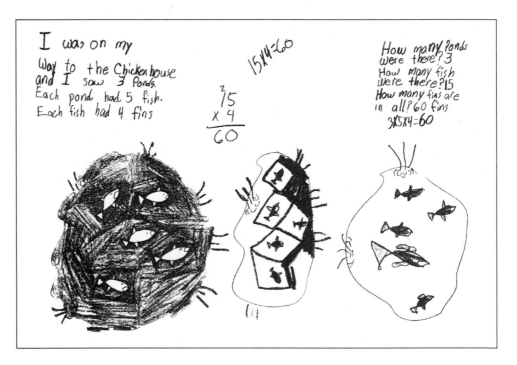

Colin connected multiplication to three ponds, each pond with five fish, and each fish with four fins.

Some students began by discussing their story ideas with other students, some began writing immediately, and others collected colored pens or crayons.

This activity gave the children an opportunity to think about multiplication in a way that made sense to them, one that was connected to things that were familiar to them. This was especially true for Macon. When I approached his desk, he was busy drawing pictures of Segas and bits and games. Macon was a Nintendo fan.

"How's it going, Macon?" I asked him.

"This is fun," he replied. "I play Nintendo all the time, and I like writing multiplication stories about the games."

"Can you explain your story to me?" I asked.

"These are 10 Segas, and these are the 18 games each Sega has," he said. "Each game has 16 bits."

"What's a bit?" I asked, exposing my complete ignorance of video games.

"A bit is like the power each game has," Macon explained. "I multiplied 10 times 16 and got 160. I knew it was 160 because I added a zero to 16 for another hundred. Then I multiplied 160 times 18 on the calculator and got 2,880 bits in all."

Aileen was drawing a large fire engine when I reached her table. "Aileen, tell me about your story," I said.

Aileen read what she had written: *"On my way to the fire Station I Saw 3 fire engines on each of the fire engines I Saw 4 dalmations on each of the dalmations I Saw 7 Spots. How many firengingines did I See? 3 How many dalmations? 12 How many Spots? 84."* After multiplying 3 by 4 in her head, Aileen used the traditional algorithm for multiplying a two-digit by one-digit number and got the answer of 84.

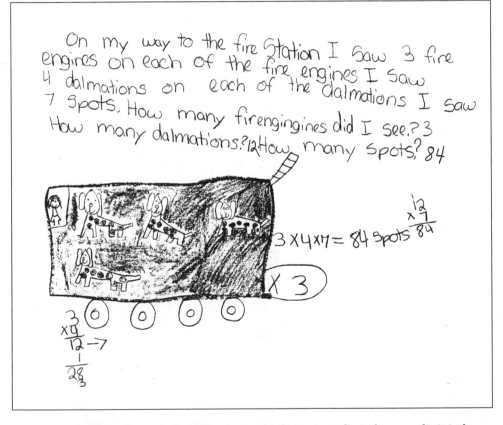

Aileen used the traditional algorithm for multiplying two digits by one digit in her story about fire engines, dalmations, and spots.

The stories the children wrote were wonderful. The topics included ant farms, castles, ornaments on Christmas trees, salt on potato chips, and feathers on turkeys. The students enjoyed listening to one another's multiplication stories and figuring the answers. They were fascinated by how large some of the answers were, and I was impressed with the size of their imaginations!

On my way to the castle I saw three bridges. On each bridge I saw 3 cars, In each car there was two radios. :) How many bridges were ther? 3, How many cars were there? 9, How many radios are there all together? 18.

$3 \times 1 = 3$

$3 \times 3 = 9$

$9 \times 2 = 18$ radios

Joss's illustration helped him solve his multiplication story.

Esio Trot

Esio Trot by Roald Dahl tells the story of two elderly people, Mr. Hoppy and Mrs. Silver, who talk to each other from their apartment balconies. Mrs. Silver loves her pet tortoise but wants it to grow larger. In hopes of winning over Mrs. Silver so she'll marry him, Mr. Hoppy gives her magic words to say to make the tortoise grow, then goes to a pet store and purchases 140 tortoises of various sizes. As time passes, he replaces the tortoises one by one, each time with one that's a little larger. The ecstatic Mrs. Silver invites Mr. Hoppy over to see how her tortoise "grew." When he asks, she agrees to marry him and they live "very happily ever after." Longer than a picture book, *Esio Trot* can be read over several days. It leads to several division problems for fourth, fifth, and sixth graders to solve.

Materials:
Optional
calculators
1 per pair of
students

The students in my fourth grade class watched intently as I held up a picture from *Esio Trot*. The illustration, by Quentin Blake, shows Mr. Hoppy gingerly making his way through a room full of tortoises, being very careful not to step on any of them. The students listened intently as I began reading the story.

I read the book over four days, reading about 10 to 12 pages each day. On the second day, I stopped on page 30 after I read the part where Mr. Hoppy buys 140 tortoises and takes them home in a basket, 10 or 15 at a time. I posed a question.

"I wonder how many trips to the pet store Mr. Hoppy would have to make if he took home 15 tortoises each time?" I asked.

Although I saw this as a division situation, I didn't mention the word *division* when I presented the problem or tell the students that they were to divide 140 by 15. The students hadn't as yet had a great deal of experience with division, and I was curious to find out whether they would see this as a situation that called for dividing. I also was curious to see how they would figure out the answer.

"Does anyone have an idea of how to go about solving this problem?" I asked.

Sebastian raised his hand. "You could keep adding 15 until you get to 140. Then you would know how many trips he took."

Amelia had another idea. "You could count by 15s until you got to 140 tortoises."

Miles chimed in, "I think it's a divide problem."

Annie said, "I think you can use take away if you start with 140 tortoises."

After the students had shared their ideas for solving the problem, I explained to them what I wanted them to do. "First, make an estimate of how many trips you think it would take. Then solve the problem, and write about how you did it. Use words and numbers to explain your reasoning, and also use pictures, if they help describe your thinking." I finished my instructions by telling the students that they had a choice as to how they would work—with a partner, in a small group, or by themselves.

Some students decided to pair up with friends, and some chose to work alone. After the children had begun to work, I made my way around the room. I wanted to make myself available to those who needed help and to answer any of their questions about the task.

Sebastian immediately calculated in his head, then ran up to me and said, "This won't work because if he took nine trips, that would be 135 tortoises, and he would still have 5 left."

I responded, "Think about what to do with those 5 tortoises."

Sebastian decided that an extra trip would have to be made and that carrying 5 tortoises was okay for Mr. Hoppy to do. Having solved the problem so quickly, Sebastian was ready for the other question I had in mind.

"When you finish writing about this problem," I said, "try figuring out how many trips Mr. Hoppy would have to take if he could carry only 10 tortoises at a time." I left Sebastian and made my way to the next table of students.

Heidi seemed frustrated. She had begun by working alone. When she realized she was stuck, however, she began discussing the problem with Ilene, who was sitting next to her. Ilene suggested that they "imagine Mr. Hoppy carrying 15 tortoises at a time from the pet store to his house." This seemed to help. Heidi wrote *140,* subtracted 15, and kept subtracting 15 until she reached 5. Then she had to subtract another 5 to get to zero. As Heidi subtracted, Ilene used the results of Heidi's calculations and recorded the number of tortoises left after each trip.

Amelia was busy counting by 15s. I listened as she said aloud each number she got after adding 15 more in her head. I was impressed at how easily Amelia added mentally. On her paper, she recorded 15, 30, 45, 60, 75, and so on up to 135. Then she jumped to 140. She wrote: *I counted like this to get my answer, and my answer is 10 trips.*

Alice estimated that it would take 50 trips. After discussing her estimate with a friend, she changed it to 15 trips. Then she multiplied 140 tortoises by 15 trips and got 2,100 trips!

"Does that seem reasonable?" I asked her.

Alice's number sense rescued her for the moment. "No way!" she responded.

I suggested that she talk to her partner about another way to solve the problem. When I left Alice to move on to another student, I noticed that she was still struggling to make sense of the numbers. (Alice eventually solved the problem by adding 15s together until she got the answer.)

Miles was the only one to use the word *divide* in his writing. He wrote: *If you dieved 140 and 15 it will eqole 9.3333333 and I don't think that's the answer.*

Although to divide was his initial instinct, when he did so on the calculator, he couldn't make sense of the decimal point and all those 3s! He didn't realize that he was on the right track. I encouraged Miles to set aside his calculator answer for a moment and try to look at the problem a different way.

"What you're telling me," I said, "is that the answer you got on the calculator doesn't make sense to you. Can you think of another method to use in order to solve the problem?"

Miles ended up adding 15s until he reached 135. "The answer is nine trips after all," he told me, "but that's only 135 tortoises, so you need to add 5 more tortoises and one more trip and you get the answer."

"I could tell that 10 was the answer from the number you got when you divided on the calculator," I told Miles.

"How?" he asked me.

"What was the number on the calculator?" I asked.

"It was this," Miles said, showing me the 9.3333333 on his paper.

"That's a number that's more than 9, but not as much as 10," I explained. "The decimal point after the 9 and the numbers that follow it tell me that."

"That's neat," Miles said.

"Suppose you divided 9 by 2," I said. "What would you get?"

"On the calculator?" Miles asked.

"Try it in your head first," I answered. "Then you can see what the calculator result would be."

Miles thought for a moment. "It's $4\frac{1}{2}$," he said.

"Yes," I agreed, "and $4\frac{1}{2}$ is a number that's more than 4 and less than 5. Try dividing 9 by 2 on the calculator."

Miles did so. "Look!" he said, excited. "It's 4.5!"

I'm not sure what Miles really understood or would remember from my explanation, but I thought the digression had potential value. Much of learning happens incidentally when a need arises, and I took this opportunity to try to give Miles a new insight.

When the students finished their work, I had them meet in a circle on the rug and take turns sharing their ideas. Some of the students reported in pairs, giving details about how they worked together by giving each other ideas or taking turns recording information and counting tortoises. Others read their individual pieces, some describing how they added in their heads, some telling how they subtracted, and others reporting how they used a calculator.

Having students share their mathematical ideas both before and after the actual work time helps in two ways. Brainstorming ideas beforehand allows children to hear different ways to approach the problem. Sharing answers and strategies afterward reinforces the idea that there are many ways to solve a problem and also helps build a sense of community in the classroom.

As our meeting on the rug came to a close, I asked the children the same question I had asked Sebastian earlier. "What if Mr. Hoppy could carry only 10 tortoises home at a time? How many trips would that be?" Some students were interested in tackling this problem, while others were more interested in hearing the rest of the story to find out exactly what Mr. Hoppy was going to do with 140 tortoises. I continued reading and left the problem for those who were interested to solve later.

The students loved the book. They especially enjoyed writing notes to one another in tortoise language, and some became quite adept at spelling words backwards. They laughed at how gullible Mrs. Silver was and waited with anticipation to find out whether Mr. Hoppy's plan to marry Mrs. Silver would really work. They were pleased to find out that Mr. Hoppy and Mrs. Silver did marry and lived "very happily ever after."

Amelia counted by 15s and then by 10s to figure out the number of trips Mr. Hoppy would have to take.

> I counted like this to get my answer and my anwer is 10
>
> 15, 30, 45, 60, 75, 90, 105, 120, 135, 140
>
> And I counted by tens like this to get my answer and it is 14
>
> 10, 20, 30, 40, 50, 60, 70, 80, 90, 100, 110, 120, 130, 140.

Jasper used addition to solve the two problems.

> How many trips will you have to take if you have 140 tortoise's and take 15 at a time.
>
> 15   60   105   150
> +15   +15   +15   -10
> ──   ──   ──   ───
> 30   75   120   140
> +15   +15   +15
> ──   ──   ──
> 45   90   135
> +15   +15   +15
> ──   ──   ──
> 60   105   150
>
> THE Amount Of trips is 10.
>
> p.s. I did not use a calculater.
>
> ───────────────────────────
>
> How many trips with 10 tortoise's if you have 140 tortoise's?
>
> 10   50   80   100   130
> +10   +10   +10   +10   +10
> ──   ──   ──   ───   ───
> 20   60   90   110   140
> +10   +10   +10   +10
> ──   ──   ──   ───
> 30   70   100   120
> +10   +10   +10
> ──   ──   100   ───
> 40   80   130
> +10
> ──
> 50
>
> THE Amont of times is 14.

From a Fifth and Sixth Grade Class

The fifth and sixth graders in Patti Reynolds's class had already read *Esio Trot* and were excited to introduce me to their class pet, a red slider turtle. After discussing the differences between red sliders and tortoises, I reminded the students about Mr. Hoppy buying 140 tortoises and taking them home 10 or 15 at a time. I then posed a slightly different version of the problem I had presented to my class.

"What's the greatest number of trips Mr. Hoppy would have to make to carry the tortoises home?" I asked. "Figure this out and explain your thinking in writing. Are there any questions?"

"How many baskets does he have?" asked Dale.

"He has one basket," I replied.

"So he can take 10 or 15. Can he take a combination, like 10 one time and 15 another time?" Liora asked.

"Yes," I answered. "He takes 10 or 15 tortoises home on each trip," I answered.

"What about the size of the tortoises?" asked Dale.

"Don't worry about size. The basket is large enough to hold 10 or 15 tortoises. Just figure out the most number of trips Mr. Hoppy would have to take," I said.

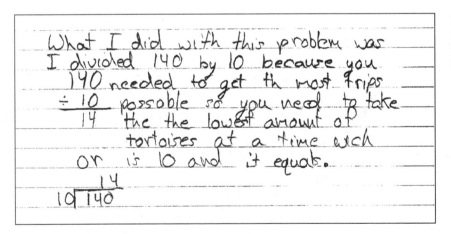

Erica divided to figure out the greatest number of trips Mr. Hoppy could take.

After about 15 minutes, all of the students had found an answer. "Who would like to report how you solved the problem?" I asked. I called on Sid.

"I multiplied 10 times 14 trips and got 140," said Sid. "I think Mr. Hoppy would have to take 10 tortoises each time because if he took 15 tortoises, then that would be fewer trips."

"Did anyone solve it a different way?" I asked.

"I think it will take 14 turns because if you divide 140 and 10 you get 14 trips," explained Emanuel. He then added, "I've read that book before, and I think it's a good book."

"Did anyone solve the problem a different way?" I asked. No one raised a hand. Everyone agreed that the most trips Mr. Hoppy would have to take would be 14.

Keith used multiplication to determine that Mr. Hoppy would have to take 14 trips.

I did 14 x 10 because 100 is 10x10 you get 100 but if you add 4 to get 14 than you x 14 by 10 and you get 140. That was the most drops.

$$\begin{array}{r} 14 \\ \times\ 10 \\ \hline 140 \end{array}$$

It would be the most because you would be Knaming all of 15 in the basket it would take you as long.

30+30+30+30+20=140
50+30+30+30=140

"I have another problem for you to solve now," I told the class.

"I bet I know," Mallory said. "I bet you're going to ask us to figure out the smallest number of trips he could make."

"I think you'll ask us how much each one cost," said Annie.

"I think you'll ask us how long it took Mr. Hoppy to carry all of the tortoises," Moss guessed.

"Or something about the size of the tortoises, like their weight," said Ursula.

"All of these are interesting problems to investigate," I responded. "The problem I'd like you to work on now starts like Mallory's: Can Mr. Hoppy get the tortoises home in fewer than 14 trips? But I'd also like you to figure out how many different ways Mr. Hoppy can get the tortoises home."

"I don't get it," Mason said.

I continued, "We know that one way is for Mr. Hoppy to take 10 tortoises at a time, which makes 14 trips. But as Liora said before, he can take home 10 on some trips and 15 on others. If he still takes 10 or 15 tortoises at a time, how many different ways can he get them all home?"

As I watched the students work, I noticed that they were solving the problem in many different ways. Some were using multiplication, and others were using division or addition. Some organized their findings into charts. Some were looking for patterns. After about 30 minutes, I stopped the students and asked for their attention.

"Some of you are at a point where you think you've found all of the ways Mr. Hoppy can take his tortoises home. What I want you to do is write a convincing argument explaining how you know you've found all the ways," I told them.

The students went back to work. I interrupted them after about 15 minutes. "I'd like us to have a mathematical conversation about what you've discovered so far," I said. "Who would like to share their thinking about the problem?"

Jackson used a chart to represent the ways to carry home the tortoises and explained the pattern he saw.

"There are five different ways I found," said Reed. "Mr. Hoppy can take the tortoises home in 14 trips, 13 trips, 12, 11, and 10 trips. I made a chart that has two columns. One column says 'Combinations' and the other column says 'Number of Trips.' So when Mr. Hoppy takes the tortoises home in 14 trips, he takes 10 tortoises every time. When he takes them home in 13 trips, there are 11 groups of 10 tortoises and 2 groups of 15. For 12 trips, there are 8 groups of 10 tortoises and 4 groups of 15. For 11 trips, there are 5 groups of

10 and 6 groups of 15 tortoises. For 10 trips, there are 2 groups of 10 and 8 groups of 15 tortoises. I noticed that on the trips where I used 15, there was an even amount of 15s." I had Reed reproduce his chart on the board.

Combinations	# of trips
10=14 15=0	14
10=11 15=2	13
10=2 15=8	10
10= 8 15= 4	12
10= 5 15= 6	11

"How could knowing about the pattern you found about even groups of 15 help you know you found all the ways?" I asked.

"Well, I know because odd numbers of 15 tortoises don't work, so I can get rid of those," he explained. "Then I just have to find the greatest even number of 15s that works for 140 and add all the 10s!"

Lexie looked at the problem differently. "The pattern I saw was this," she said. "If you see the times you use 15 tortoises, it goes 15 times 2, 15 times 4, 15 times 6, 15 times 8. See the number on the right is a pattern like 2, 4, 6, 8. But if you go to 10 you get 150 tortoises, and that's too many. The pattern is over, so that's how I know I have all the ways."

"How come Mr. Hoppy can't take 15 tortoises three times, or five times, or seven times?" I asked.

"If you use an uneven number of 15 tortoises you get a remainder," said Erica.

"Can you give us an example?" I asked.

"If Mr. Hoppy takes three groups of 15 tortoises, that's 45 tortoises," explained Amelia. "He would have to take 10 groups of 10, but that makes 145 tortoises. If he took nine groups of 10, the total would be 135 tortoises, with 5 remaining."

"I did it by adding," said Moss. "I started with the most number of trips, zero groups of 15 plus 140. Then I did 30 plus 110, 60 plus 80, 90 plus 50, 120 plus 20. I noticed the numbers on the left go up by 30 each time, like this: 0, 30, 60, 90, 120. The numbers on the right go down by 30 each time, like this: 140, 110, 80, 50, 20."

"Looking at the number patterns seems to have helped some of you be sure that you have found all the ways," I said.

"I know I have all the ways because I tried all the numbers and combinations on paper and the calculator," Liora said.

"I wonder if you could change the numbers around, how many different combinations would there be?" asked Caitlin.

"Do you mean if the order were important?" I asked.

"Yes," said Caitlin. "To get 140 tortoises home, Mr. Hoppy could take them in 11 trips by taking 6 groups of 15 tortoises and 5 groups of 10. But what if he took 15 tortoises on the first trip, 10 the second, and 15 the third. Or he could take 10 tortoises on the first trip, and 15 on the second trip, and so on. What if the order counted? How many ways would there be?"

"That would be a huge problem!" exclaimed Jackson.

After the students shared the different ways they had solved the tortoise problem, I continued reading the story. When the students found out that Mrs. Silver would marry Mr. Hoppy, they applauded. It was their way of congratulating Mr. and Mrs. Hoppy and showing their appreciation for a book they enjoyed.

These are the other ways that he could take 140 tortoises home without there being any leftovers

| 15 |
| 15 |
| 10 |
| 10 |
| 10 |
| 10 | 13 trips |
| 10 |
| 10 |
| 10 |
| 10 |
| 10 |
| 10 |
| + 10 |
| 140 tortoises |

How many 15's you have it has to be an even number because if you didn't then you would end up with leftovers.

Convincing Arguament

2	3	4
15	15	15
15	15	15
15	15	15
15	15	15
10	15	15
10	15	15
10	10	15
10	10	15
10	10	10
10	10	10
10	10	10
10		10
10		

Altogether there are 5 ways that he could take 140 tortoises home. I know this because every time I went to another way I would always add 2 more 15's because like I said you have to have an even →

number of 15's. So once I had 8 15's I knew that that was as high a I could go because I knew that every time I added 2 15's, it was like adding 30, so when I had 8 15's I only had 2 10's, and that equals 20, so I couldn't add 2 more 15's.

Pablo added combinations of 10s and 15s to find all the ways to carry 140 tortoises.

The Giraffe That Walked to Paris

Nancy Milton's *The Giraffe That Walked to Paris* tells the true story of a giraffe that the pasha of Egypt gave to the king of France in 1826. The giraffe traveled by ship to Marseilles, then on foot through the towns and villages of France, all the way to Paris. Along the way, the giraffe created a sensation, for French people had never seen this type of animal before. At the end of the book, the author provides more historical information and includes a map that shows the long distance the giraffe traveled—1,700 miles by sea and 425 miles on foot. Students figure out the average time it takes to walk 1 mile, then estimate how long it would take them to walk 425 miles.

"This is a true story about a giraffe that lived a long time ago," I told Carole Smith's fourth and fifth graders as I began the lesson. I showed the class the book and said, "The book is called *The Giraffe That Walked to Paris*, and it's written by Nancy Milton. The story takes place in the year 1826. How long ago was that? See if you can figure this out mentally." This was 1995, and the problem was a challenge for the class.

After about a minute, several hands shot up. I waited until about half of the students had raised their hands, and then I called on Jo.

"I think it was 169 years ago," she said. "I started at 1826 and added 100 to get to 1926. Then I added by 10s from 26 to 96 and that was 70. Then I took 1 year away to get 169." There was a buzz of reaction. Some students nodded in agreement; others looked puzzled. I gave them a few moments to talk with one another, and then I called them back to attention.

"Did anyone solve it in a different way?" I asked. I called on Aubrey.

"I saw 1995 minus 1826 in my head and I just did subtraction," he explained. "I got 169 years ago as the answer."

"I just subtracted 26 from 95 and got 69," said Eden. "Then I just added on 100 more because it was the 1800s and we're in the 1900s. I got 169."

"This story takes place 169 years ago in Egypt and France," I then said. I walked over to the world map, pulled it down, and pointed to the two countries.

I continued, "I'm going to read part of the story to you, and then I'll stop to ask you some mathematical questions."

The students were fascinated by the giraffe's journey from Egypt to Paris and seemed interested in every detail about life in nineteenth-century

France. They especially liked the illustration of the giraffe wearing a raincoat, buttoned up and with a hood, standing next to Professor Saint-Hilaire, who had made the coat and was going to lead the giraffe to Paris.

I read the story up to the part where Professor Saint-Hilaire and the giraffe arrive in Paris. "At 5 p.m. on June 30, 1827, Professor Saint-Hilaire led the giraffe into her new home: a yard in the Paris zoo." I deliberately stopped before the author reveals exactly how many days it took the giraffe to walk to Paris. I skipped to the back of the book to show the class a map of the giraffe's journey.

"This map shows the giraffe's journey from Marseilles to Paris," I said. "It indicates that the journey on foot was about 425 miles. I wonder how long it would take us to walk that far? What would you need to know in order to find out?"

"You'd need to know how long it would take you to walk a mile," said Flint. "I think if you started with a mile it would be easier."

Flint's suggestion led me in the direction I had planned. I said, "Before we think further about how long it would take us to walk 425 miles as the giraffe did, let's think about 1 mile." I wrote on the board:

How long is a mile?
How long would it take to walk a mile?
How could you measure a mile?

"Talk with the people at your table about what you know about 1 mile," I said. "Then write down all of your ideas."

Students began discussing their ideas. Some went searching for dictionaries and encyclopedias, while others reached for rulers and yardsticks. After about 10 minutes, the discussions began to wane, and the students started jotting down their thoughts. They worked hard for another 15 minutes until I asked for their attention.

"Raise your hand if you'd like to share some of your ideas about 1 mile," I said. I called on Jonah.

"We think it would take about 45 minutes to go 1 mile walking on flat ground," he said. "You could use a measuring tape, a ruler, or a yardstick to measure out a mile."

Judy reported next. "We looked up a mile in the dictionary and it said that it's 5,280 feet," she said. "I think it would take about 15 minutes to walk a mile. I think you could measure a mile by walking around the school track."

"We agree with Jonah that it would take 45 minutes to walk a mile," said Jed. "You could measure it with a car."

"Yes," I said, "every car has an odometer that measures the distance in miles."

"I'd use landmarks to figure a mile, like the signs on the freeway," suggested Calie. "Or I could count my footsteps."

"When you go home this afternoon," I said, "I'd like you to continue thinking about how long a mile is and how you can measure it. If you can, try walking a mile, and see how long it takes you. Also, discuss this with your parents and continue writing down the ideas you get."

Giving the students this assignment was a way to link math homework to the real world. I wanted the students to experience what a mile was before I asked them to figure out how long it would take them to walk 425 miles.

Jed clustered his ideas about the length of a mile.

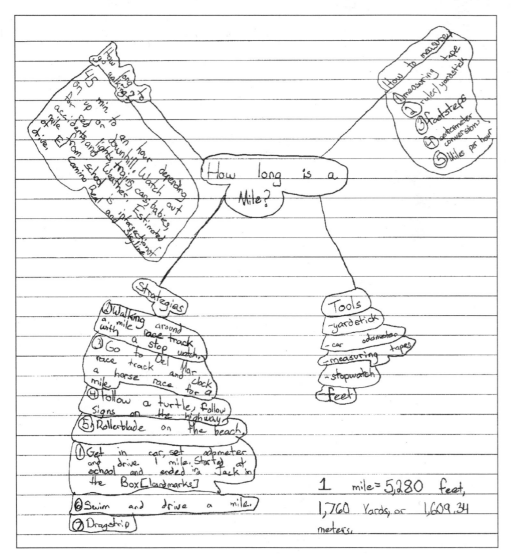

The Second Day

To begin the second day of our investigation, I said, "Share what you discovered about 1 mile with the others at your table." Having students talk about what they learned is especially beneficial to those who don't do the homework. After several minutes, I asked for volunteers to report to the class.

"I learned that walking from the beach to the school is close to a mile because my mom and I measured it in our car," said Deirdre.

"I measured how long a mile is by getting two orange cones," said Wesley. "I put an odometer on my bike, then set a cone down. I rode the bike until it showed a mile on the odometer, then I put the other cone down."

If I had to mesher how long a mile is, I would get two orang cones a bike and an odomiter, Hook the odomiter up to the bike then set a cone down. Ride the bike untile is shows a mile stop and set the other cone down there then meshur how long a mile is

Wesley found a practical way to determine the length of a mile.

"I was thinking of using a yardstick and laying it down and measuring out 1,760 yards, but I had to eat dinner and I didn't have time," Jo reported.

"I estimated that a mile is from Foussat Street to Crouch Street," said Calie.

"My dad says that from school to the bottom of Hinie Hills is a mile," Judy said.

"Mile-High Stadium in Denver is a mile high," said Maggie.

"From your homework experience, many of you have a sense of what a mile is," I said. "Yesterday, a few people suggested that we measure a mile by using our school track. I know that four times around the track equals 1 mile." Several hands shot up in the air. I called on Theo.

"I think we should walk around the track and find out how long it takes us!" he exclaimed. The class enthusiastically agreed. (Had Theo not suggested this, I would have done so.)

With stopwatch in hand, I led the class out to the field and gave instructions for walking a mile. The students were excited about this part of the investigation. Some were a little overenthusiastic and their mile "walk" was more like a mile "speed-walk." I recorded each student's walking time, and then we made our way back to the classroom.

Back in class, I gave each student a 3-by-3-inch Post-it. "Record your time on your Post-it and then put it on the board." The students quickly wrote down their times, and soon the board was filled with 29 Post-its.

"Raise your hand if you have a suggestion for organizing the data," I said. I called on Larissa.

"Put them in order from the quickest time to the slowest," she suggested.

"Other suggestions?" I asked.

"Put the same ones together in towers," Wesley said.

No one else raised a hand, so I began to rearrange the Post-its following their suggestions. Students called out times to help me.

When I finished, the Post-its indicated that the students' times ranged from 12 to 23 minutes. Many Post-its were in the 15-minute column, with the rest dispersed between 12 and 23 minutes.

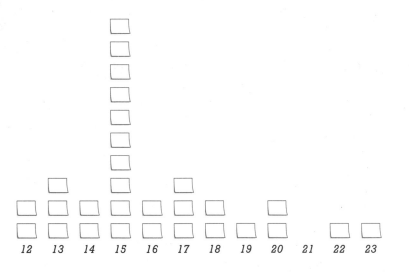

"Who can make a mathematical statement about the data?" I asked.

"It looks like a graph," said Paige.

"The times go from 12 minutes to 23 minutes," said Jed.

"There are a lot of 15s," Emily added.

"If we were to find the typical walking time for a mile for the people in this room, how might we go about it?" I asked.

"That's like the average, isn't it?" Jo asked.

"That's right," I responded.

"The mode is around 15 minutes and that's a kind of average," said Benno.

"That's right, Benno. Can anyone think of another way to figure the average?" I asked. No one raised a hand, so I decided to explain how to find the median of the class graph.

"Another kind of average is called the *median*," I said. "Mathematicians find the median by locating the data in the middle, with the same number of data above and below it." I demonstrated this by removing one Post-it at a time from each end of the graph of data, moving them down to form a new row. Finally, only one Post-it remained in the original graph. It read 15 minutes and 10 seconds.

"So that's the average speed we walked for a mile?" asked Bernardo.

"That's the median," I answered. "We could use it to say our average time was about 15 minutes."

"Yesterday I read the first part of *The Giraffe That Walked to Paris*," I reminded the class. "The giraffe walked 425 miles from Marseilles to Paris. If we wanted to walk 425 miles, where would we end up? Where in California is 425 miles from Oceanside? Discuss this with the others at your table."

"Can we use our social studies book?" asked Judy.

"Of course," I answered.

Students worked in their groups for about 5 minutes, poring over books and measuring distances with rulers. I walked from table to table, checking to see how things were going. When all the groups were ready, I called for their attention and repeated my question.

"We found out that Yosemite is about 425 miles from Oceanside," reported Jansen. "We did it with a ruler. Down here there's a scale and it's $1\frac{1}{8}$ inch for every 100 miles."

"We think Monterey is about 425 miles from here," said Jo. "We used a ruler and measured off 3 centimeters for every 100 miles off the coastline."

"We measured the same way but we ended up in Merced," said Marsala.

"We got to Salinas," Eden said.

"I started at the Salton Sea and ended up somewhere in the Sierra Nevada," said Flint, giggling.

As the students reported their findings, I wrote the names down on the board:

Yosemite, Monterey, Merced, Salinas

"Your problem is to figure out how long it would take you to walk 425 miles," I then said to the students to get them started. "You may work on this problem with a partner or in a group, but you each need to record your own work. Use the data from our class graph, the information you gathered from your homework assignment, and anything else that you think would be useful."

"Do we use the average time the class walked a mile or our own time?" Calie asked.

"That's up to you," I responded. "Remember, think about how long you would want to walk each day."

"What about sleeping time?" asked Eden.

"And what about eating and snacks and resting time?" Kendall asked.

"Yeah, and when you go up hills, you walk slower than going down hills," Camilla added.

"What other things would you have to think about?" I asked.

"People on the sidewalk may be blocking your way, like the giraffe in the story, so that would slow you down sometimes," said Jed.

There were a lot of animated discussions about how long to allow for eating, sleeping, getting tired, obstacles, walking speed, hills, and so on. The students worked together in small groups or with partners, helping each other get started.

I walked from table to table, listening in on their conversations and lending a helping hand when I was needed.

As the students completed their written explanations, I had them read to me what they had written.

Cameron read, *"Im going to sleap from 9 pm to 7 am. I would start from Oceanside and start To walk To Yosemite. My estement for hills is for every 15 feet it would slow me down 7 sec. I would walk for 14 hours But I would take off 4 hours for eating and resting so I would realy be walking for 10 hours. I would be walke 4 miles per every hour because There are 4 15's in every hour. In 10 hours I can walc 41 miles a day. I counted by fors 10 times and got 41 miles. It took me 10 days to walk 425."*

"Your explanation is clear to me," I said. "I have one question: How much is 4 times 10?"

"It's 40," Cameron responded. Then he quickly added, "I know, I know, why did I say 41? Because I stuck an extra mile in there because I'm a fast walker."

Dylan wrote: *Last summer my brother my dad and I went backpaking for three days. We walked 30 miles in thos three days. Now I know we can walk 10 miles in one day. I know that because I divided 30 by 3. I know 100 miles = 10 day. That would be about 42 days. I know that because 10 gos into 100 10 times and the 10 ecwuls [equals] days. and the 100 ecwuls miles and that would ecwul 42 days. 10 days for 100 miles 20 days for 200 miles, 30 days for 300 miles and 40 days for 400 miles and add 2 days ecwuls 425.*

Jo made a chart to figure out how many miles she would walk per day. Using the class average of 15 minutes per mile and 4 miles an hour, she organized her chart with "hours" on one side and "miles" on the other. Starting with 1 hour at 4 miles, she continued with 2 hours at 8 miles, 3 hours at 12 miles until she got to 9½ hours at 38 miles.

"How did you figure 9½ hours walking time a day?" I asked.

Because the rest of the time I'd be sleeping, and I had to figure in for other things like hills, getting tired, and eating," she replied.

"How did you figure that it would take you 12 days?" I asked.

"Because 425 miles divided by 38 miles a day equals a little over 11 days, so I figured about 12 days," she explained.

Judy read from her paper: *"I estemated my adjustment time and added them to get 13 hours and 20 minuts. Then I subtracted the hours in the day (24 hours) and my adjustment time (13 hours and 20 minutes) to get 9 hours and 20 minutes walking time a day and 13 hours and 20 minutes of adjustment time."*

"What do you mean by 'adjustment time'?" I asked.

"My adjustment times were things I'll be doing when I'm not walking or things that slow me down," she explained. "I'll spend 10 hours a day for sleeping, 2 hours a day for climbing hills, 50 minutes for obstacles, 1 hour for getting tired, and I adjusted for walking slowly 50 minutes a day. I know I can go 4 miles an hour because that's the average walking time for the class. I multiplied 4 miles times 9 hours a day and got 36 miles a day. I added an extra mile for the 20 minutes. In 12 days I would walk 444 miles."

"Your explanation gives a lot more information than you included in your paper," I commented to Judy.

"Do I have to write more?" she asked.

"Remember that your writing is supposed to explain how you reasoned," I said. "I think that you need to explain what you meant by 'adjustment time.' I think that would strengthen your paper." Judy returned to her seat and, with some reluctance, began to write some more.

Judy explained why it would take her 12 days to walk from Oceanside to Monterey.

Each time I passed by Flint and Jonah, they were experimenting with another way to solve the problem. Finally, they began to look for all of the ways to make 425 using multiplication. They decided on 5 miles × 85 days = 425 miles. They had tried 47 miles a day × 9 days, but decided that 47 miles was too far to walk in 1 day.

The conversations I heard among the students as I walked around to each table revealed the variety of ways they were thinking about the problem. For example, I overheard Judy ask Jo and Camilla, "How fast does a plane fly?"

"Why?" they responded.

"Because it takes $1\frac{1}{2}$ hours to fly to San Francisco, and that's about 400 miles. It might help me figure out how long it would take to walk to Monterey," said Judy.

"They fly 600 to 800 miles per hour," said Benno, who overheard the conversation. "I know because my dad makes airplanes."

"What answer did you get?" Anne-Marie asked Deirdre.

"I don't want to give away my answer, but I took my calculator and I multiplied 425 miles times 15 minutes and divided by 60 to get an answer in hours and then divided by 24 to get an answer in days. I'm figuring averages for obstacles, hills, and meals."

When the students finished their work, many volunteered to share their papers. They were surprised at the variety of answers and became curious about the giraffe and how long it took her to walk the 425 miles.

Finally, I returned to the story, starting where I had left off the day before. When the students learned that it had taken the giraffe 41 days to walk from Marseilles to Paris, most of them weren't surprised. They had worked long and hard on this problem, and 41 days seemed reasonable to them.

Paige thought that 7.1 miles was a reasonable distance to walk in 1 day.

How long will it take to walk 425 miles?

I think it will take me 60 days because it sounds reasonable.
I'm starting in Oceanside to Yosemite.
I know that if you walk a mile its 15 min.
I also know that I have to walk 425 miles.
So what I'm going to do is multiply 60 days
That's the closest I could come
up to.

$$\begin{array}{r} 60 \text{ days} \\ \times\ 7.1 \text{ miles} \\ \hline 426 \text{ miles} \end{array}$$

I walk 7.1 miles a day
The rest of the day I went
to sleep

Grandfather Tang's Story

In *Grandfather Tang's Story*, by Ann Tompert, Grandfather Tang and Little Soo are sitting under a tree playing with tangram puzzles when Grandfather Tang begins telling the story of two foxes who change into different animals to outdo each other. One changes into a rabbit and the other into a dog, one changes into a squirrel and the other into a hawk, and so on. With each animal, Grandfather Tang creates a matching tangram shape. This book combines a story about friendship and competition with the fascination of tangram shapes. The book is a springboard to an activity in which students make their own tangrams, then use them to investigate geometric shapes and explore area and measurement.

Materials:
6" squares of
Construction paper,
1 per student

1 large sheet
colored butcher paper

Scissors 1 per
pr student

"Tangrams are ancient Chinese puzzles that adults and children still use today," I told Carol Schurlock's sixth graders to begin the lesson. "I have a book I'd like to read to you about a storyteller who tells his granddaughter a tale using pieces of the tangram puzzle."

I began reading *Grandfather Tang's Story*. Robert Andrew Parker's watercolors captured the students' attention. They listened quietly to all of the fox's adventures and predicted what the animals would turn into as they chased after each other.

When I finished reading the story, I gave each student a 6-by-6-inch square of construction paper and a pair of scissors.

"Do we get to make tangrams?" Melanie asked.

"Yes," I answered. "We're each going to make our own set." When all of the students had the materials, I called for their attention.

"Hold up your square and fold it in half along the diagonal," I instructed. "What shape are you holding now?"

"A triangle," they responded.

"Open the triangle and cut the square in half along the diagonal," I said. I held up my square and cut it in half to show them what I meant.

"You should now have two triangles," I continued. "Put one of these triangles on your table. Take the other triangle. Fold it in half, open it up, and cut along the fold so you have two smaller triangles." I demonstrated how the students were to do this.

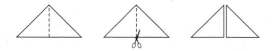

"Compare the two triangles. What do you notice about them?" I asked.

"They're exactly the same," said Josiah.

"The triangles are congruent," added Cecily, pleased to remember the word.

"How do you know they're congruent?" I asked.

"Because if you took one of them and laid it on top of the other, they're both the same size and shape," Cecily explained.

"What else do you notice about these triangles?" I asked. The students were flipping and rotating their triangles and talking to one another. Soon, several hands were wiggling in the air. I called on Deborah.

"They both have a square corner," she said. "It's a 90-degree angle." Deborah held up a triangle and pointed to the 90-degree angle with her finger.

"Show me with your index finger where the 90-degree angle is on one of your triangles," I instructed the class. Most students quickly located the 90-degree angle; a few checked with neighbors to see if they were correct.

"Mathematicians call triangles with a square corner or a 90-degree angle *right triangles,*" I added.

I continued with directions for cutting the tangram puzzle. "Put the two congruent triangles on your table and pick up the large triangle," I said. "Now, make two folds on the large triangle. First, fold it in half as you did with the other large triangle. Then take the top corner and fold it down until it touches the base of the triangle. Watch as I do this. You have to make two folds before you cut." I had the students follow as I demonstrated each fold and then opened the triangle and cut along the horizontal fold.

"Can someone tell us the names of these two shapes?" I asked.

"A triangle and a trapezoid," Jordan replied. "I learned about trapezoids last year." I nodded my agreement.

"Now take the trapezoid and cut it in half along the fold. That makes two trapezoids," I instructed.

"Fold one of the trapezoids to make a square and a triangle, open it, and cut it along the fold," I then directed. This was easy for the students to do.

"Next, fold and cut the last trapezoid to make a parallelogram and a triangle," I explained. This was the most difficult step, and I had the students follow as I demonstrated, watching carefully to see that they were folding and cutting as I was.

I walked around to each table, checking to see that the students had folded and cut correctly. When I got to Gunther's table, I noticed that he had cut his square into too many pieces. I handed him a new square from the extras I had in my pocket and reminded him that mistakes are part of learning. With assistance from his neighbor, he quickly made a correct set of tangram pieces.

When everyone had a complete set of seven tangram pieces, I asked for the children's attention. "Now that each of you has your own tangram set, make a triangle on your table," I said.

"Can we use more than one tangram piece?" Joy asked.

"Yes," I replied. The students quickly made triangles, some using one piece, some two or more. I then gave instructions for the next part of the lesson.

"In the story, the foxes changed into different animals," I said. "Take the triangle you've made and change it into another triangle, then another, then another, using different pieces. Work with the people in your group and make as many different triangles as you can."

"How will we keep track of them?" asked Deborah.

"Once you've made a triangle, trace it on a piece of paper and cut it out," I explained. I pointed to a large sheet of blue butcher paper on the board. "When everyone is finished, we'll post examples of all the different triangles you found."

"When we're tracing, do we trace around each piece or just the whole triangle?" asked Marlon.

"Trace around each piece, so we can see how you made each triangle," I replied.

The students worked in their groups cooperatively, helping one another put tangram pieces together to make different triangles. I noticed that there were discussions about other shapes they encountered as they searched for triangles. A few students colored their triangles, and the idea spread throughout the class. Soon, most of them were busily coloring before they cut. After about 30 minutes, I asked for their attention.

"I'd like to have all the different triangles you found posted on the blue paper," I told them. "We'll take turns so that one group at a time posts a triangle. Choose one person from your group to do the posting. Remember that we want to post triangles that are all different."

"I have a question," said Deborah. "Are these two triangles different?" She held up two triangles that were the same size and shape, both made from all seven pieces, but the arrangements of the pieces were different.

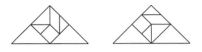

"What do you think?" I asked.

"Well, I think they're different because the pieces are in different places," Deborah answered.

"I agree," I responded. "There can be different arrangements of the same tangram pieces."

The students watched as one group after another brought a triangle up to the front of the room to post. Some students carefully held their triangles next to others on the chart to see if they were the same or different. When Frasier posted a triangle that was the same as one already posted, several hands went up.

"Frasier's is the same as the other triangle made from three pieces!" Skye exclaimed. "He used the same pieces and the same arrangement." Frasier held his triangle next to the one Skye was referring to. He studied the two triangles and realized that they were identical.

Soon the blue paper was covered with triangles made from one, two, three, four, and seven tangram pieces.

"Let's take a look at our collection of triangles," I said. "When mathematicians want to make better sense of information, they organize it. Raise your hand if you have an idea about how we could organize the triangles." I called on Lyric.

"We could make a list of the number of pieces across the board," she said. "That would be 1 to 7. Then we could put the triangles made from one piece under that heading, ones with two pieces under the two-piece heading, and so on."

"Does anyone else have an idea for organizing the triangles?" I asked. No one raised a hand. I quickly rearranged the triangles, following Lyric's directions.

"We don't have any triangles made with six tangram pieces," Gunther noticed.

"There's no triangles made with five pieces either," Roxanne added.

The students went back to work, searching for ways to make new triangles for the class chart.

"I think I have another triangle with seven tangram pieces," said Augie. He brought his triangle up to the chart and studied the shapes.

"Augie, yours is the same as that one," said Nico, pointing to another triangle made from seven tangram pieces. "Why don't you put your triangle next to that one and see?" Augie tested his triangle and found that it wasn't different. He quickly returned to his seat to try another idea. He soon made a triangle using five pieces. Others cheered when he posted it.

Lyric found a triangle made of three pieces that was different from the two posted. "Yes!" she said, grinning as she posted it.

"I think I've got one for six tangram pieces!" Claire shouted. Several students ran over to her desk. Running was not usually allowed in Mrs. Schurlock's class, but even Carole Schurlock found herself rushing over to Claire's desk to see what all the excitement was about.

"Oh, she accidentally used another medium-sized triangle from someone else's set," said Jarvis, disappointed. Undaunted, Claire went right back to work.

Some students were gathered at another table, watching someone work. I peeked over their shoulders and found Jordan working feverishly to put six tangram pieces together.

"I've got it!" he exclaimed. He quickly traced and cut out his discovery, and then posted it on the class chart. Melanie and Frasier also made triangles from the same six pieces that Jordan used, but theirs were different arrangements of the pieces. They posted them.

I called the class to attention. "I'd like everyone to take a look at the class chart and talk with someone next to you about what you notice," I told them. After a minute or so, several students had their hands raised. I called on Curt.

"They're all triangles," he said.

"Some are the same size but they're still different," said Alexandra. "Like those two triangles are both made from four pieces, but they have different pieces." She went up to the chart to prove it to the class.

"Well, a lot of them are congruent, really," Deborah said.

"Tell us what you mean, Deborah," I said.

"If you just look at the size and not the position of the pieces inside, then a lot of them are congruent," she explained. "Like, all of the seven-piece triangles and six-piece triangles."

"The triangles made from one tangram piece are all different sizes," added Gunther.

"Let's take a look at the triangles Gunther is talking about," I said, pointing to the three triangles made from single tangram pieces. "Because these triangles aren't the same size, they aren't congruent."

I posed another question. "Look at all the triangles. How else are they different?"

"They have different areas," said Ryan.

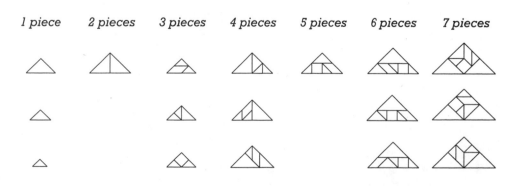

| 1 piece | 2 pieces | 3 pieces | 4 pieces | 5 pieces | 6 pieces | 7 pieces |

"Let's say that the square piece is worth 1 unit of area," I said. "Take one of the other tangram pieces, and figure out what its area is. Check with your neighbor." While most of the students were able to figure the area of a piece, a few checked with their neighbors for help.

"What's the area of the small triangle?" I asked.

"One-half," responded some of the students.

"That's easy," several said.

"If the square is worth 1 unit of area, what's the value of the parallelogram?" I asked. This was not as easy. The students talked about this in their groups for a bit, and then several hands shot up.

"I think the parallelogram is worth 1 unit because you can fit two small triangles on top of it," explained Frasier. "Since the small triangles are worth ½, I added ½ plus ½ and it makes 1 whole."

"What about the large triangle?" I asked. I gave them time to think and then called on Lyric.

"The large triangle is worth 2 units," she said.

"How do you know?" I asked her.

"Because four small triangles fit on it," Lyric replied. "I know that if you add ½ plus ½ plus ½ plus ½, it equals 2."

"And the medium-size triangle?" I asked.

"It's the same as the square," Alexandra said. "You can prove it by matching two small triangles on top of it."

"Now that you know the value of each piece, I have a problem for you to solve," I said. "I want you to choose a triangle with at least two pieces from our class chart. Use your tangram pieces to make that triangle, then trace it onto a sheet of white paper. Then figure the area of your triangle if the square is worth 1 unit of area. Remember to explain your thinking using words and numbers. You can work together and help one another, but each of you needs to record individually."

The students were excited about the problem. I distributed sheets of 8½-by-11-inch white paper, and the students began tracing triangles. After a few minutes, everyone was working hard to figure the area of his or her triangle.

Raven read to me how she figured the area: *"To find the area you need to add each shape and since a square equals 1 so you would measure the square with all the shapes and the small triangle equals ½ and the medium triangle equals 1 and the large triangle equals 2 and the other small triangle equals ½ and then you add it all up and you get 4. ½ + 1 + 2 + ½ = 4."*

Ryan explained in writing how he solved the problem: *I think this triangle equals 8 because you can get a hole square and put it on the triangl 6 times, but ther are four halfes left over put 2 halfes together and you get a hole then do the same with the other two and its a hole, and those two pluse the other 6 is 8.*

As the students finished, I gave them the challenge of figuring the area of their triangle when the value of the square was ½ or ¼.

Again, Ryan explained how he figured the area of his triangle when the value of the square was ¼: *If the squar is worth ¼ than the triangle is worth two because you need ⁴⁄₄ in order to make a hole, and in the triangle ¼ goes* *into it 8 times. . . . If you have $\frac{4}{4}$ it is a hole and the other $\frac{4}{4}$ equal 1 hole than that makes 1 hole + 1 hole = 2 holes and the value is two.*

Lyric read from her paper: *"If the square is one forth the whole triangle is worth 1. It is one because the big triangle is worth $\frac{1}{2}$ + the medium triangle which is $\frac{1}{4}$ + $\frac{2}{8}$ or $\frac{1}{4}$ from the two small triangles equals 1."*

When the students were finished, we worked together to record the areas of all the triangles on the class chart using the square as 1 unit of area.

"Now that you know the areas of the triangles on our chart, raise your hand if you have any questions, comments, or observations," I said.

"All the triangles made from seven pieces have the same area," said Lyric.

"That's also true for the triangles made from six pieces," added Alec.

"There are three different triangles made from four pieces," said Jordan. "Two of them have areas of 4 and the other one has an area of $4\frac{1}{2}$; it's a little bigger."

"It's weird that the triangle made from five pieces has the same area as two of them made from four pieces," Deborah said.

"The more pieces you use the greater the area, except for one or two triangles," said Ryan.

"I wonder what a pentagon chart would look like?" Claire inquired. "I wonder if we could find more pentagons than triangles?"

"That would be interesting," I said. "We can investigate pentagons on another day."

This activity gave the students a chance to see mathematics in a way that integrated several topics. It not only gave them the chance to explore how geometric shapes can be put together in different ways, but it also linked a geometry experience to the areas of number and measurement. Also, the activity gave the students the opportunity to think about fractions.

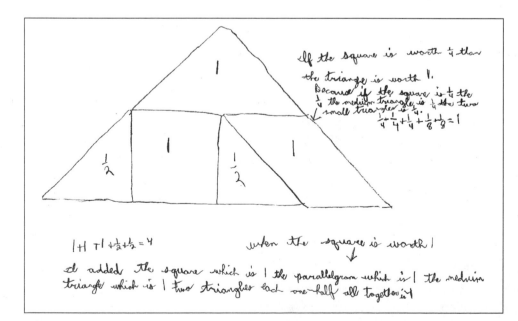

Marius chose a five-piece triangle and figured the areas when the square was worth $\frac{1}{4}$ and when it was worth 1.

Is a Blue Whale the Biggest Thing There Is?

Materials:

1 ball of yarn at least 100 feet long

yardsticks and tape measures 1 each per group of 4 students

3" x 3" sticky notes, 1 per student

> In *Is a Blue Whale the Biggest Thing There Is?* author and illustrator Robert E. Wells gives readers an incredible look at the size of things in the world around us. The book starts by introducing the largest creature on earth: the blue whale, which can grow to be 100 feet long. Then the book shows that a tower of jars, each filled with 100 blue whales, "would look quite small balanced on top of Mount Everest!" Mount Everest is compared to Earth, Earth to the sun, the sun to "a red supergiant star called Antares," Antares to our galaxy, and galaxies to the universe. After reading the book, students complete activities that involve measuring, finding averages, and comparing lengths.

"A blue whale can grow to be 100 feet long and weigh 150 tons!" Patty Montgomery read as she showed her fourth graders a picture of a blue whale from *Is a Blue Whale the Biggest Thing There Is?*

The children were fascinated by the size comparisons throughout the book. The picture of an enormous jar of 100 blue whales next to an elephant, a horse, and a lion drew "oohs" and "aahs." Another picture of a tiny bag of 100 full-sized Earths orbiting around a gigantic sun prompted exclamations of disbelief. The students were amazed that more than 1 million Earths would equal the size of the sun, and that more than 50 million suns would equal the size of Antares, "a red supergiant star."

When she finished reading the book, Patty turned back to the page showing the picture of the blue whale.

"In the book it says that blue whales can reach 100 feet in length," said Patty. "How long do you think 100 feet is?"

"About as long as the field outside," said Amon.

"I think it's longer than our classroom," offered Kira.

To demonstrate a length of 100 feet, Patty used a yardstick and a ball of yarn. "Since there are 3 feet in a yard," she said, "let's count by 3s as I measure." As Patty measured the yarn 1 yard at a time, one student rolled the yarn back into a ball so it wouldn't get tangled.

When Patty had measured 4 yards and the students had counted to 12 feet, Patty asked, "Will we land on 100 feet if we continue counting by 3s?"

"No," said Amika. "We'll say 99, then 102."

After the class had counted by 3s to 99, Patty measured one more foot of yarn to equal 100 feet. She then cut the yarn.

"If we stretch out this 100-foot yarn across the room, how would it compare to the length of the room?" asked Patty.

Students called out several answers. "It's longer." "It would go much farther." "It's a lot more."

"How about through this room, the next room, and onto the playground?" she asked. This time, most of the students were unsure.

Patty took the class into the hall. The students helped unravel the yarn by standing a few feet apart in a long line and holding the yarn at their waists.

"This is the length of a blue whale," Patty reminded them. "Try to keep this picture in your mind."

The students then rolled the yarn back up and returned to the classroom. Patty posed a question.

"How many fourth graders do you think it would take to equal a blue whale's length of 100 feet?" she asked.

"Do you mean lying down end to end or standing next to each other?" Gideon asked.

"Lying down end to end," Patty replied. "Discuss this in your groups and decide on an estimate."

After a few minutes, Patty repeated the question and had the groups report their estimates. The students at Table 1 couldn't agree. They each had come up with a different estimate—40, 50, 80, and 100.

"How tall would each student be if 100 students equaled 100 feet?" Patty asked, to help the students think about whether their estimates were reasonable.

"Only 1 foot tall," said Derek.

"Is that possible?" Patty asked.

"No!" the students chorused.

Patty thanked Table 1 for giving the class an opportunity to think more about their estimates. Then she gave the students a minute or so to revise their estimates and again asked for their ideas. Now their estimates ranged from 10 to 50.

"What would you need to know to solve this problem?" Patty asked.

"Measure each person," Gina suggested.

"You have to know how many kids there are," said Kira.

"You have to picture how big a blue whale is and then picture how many kids would fit along it," said Jill.

"Maybe you could take the yarn outside again and have kids lie on it," said Gina.

"What if you weren't allowed to use the yarn?" asked Patty.

"Make up sizes for the children," replied Sawyer.

"What would be a reasonable size for a fourth grader?" Patty continued.

"Four feet tall?" Kira guessed.

"Do any of you think you are 4 feet tall?" Patty asked. Dalya raised her hand. Using the yardstick, Patty measured Dalya's height. She was just about 4 feet 2 inches tall.

"But lots of kids are taller than Dalya," Jonas said.

"What else could be a reasonable height for a fourth grader?" Patty asked.

"Maybe 4 feet 10 inches," Jonas said. He came up to the front of the group to be measured. Jonas was a little taller than 5 feet.

"I think we should have everyone measure themselves," suggested Kira. The students seemed eager to find out how tall they were.

Patty demonstrated how to measure a student's height by measuring Amon. She used one of several tape measures she had in the room. Patty had another student hold the tape at Amon's toes, and she stretched it above his head, pinching the tape where it reached the top of his head.

"Amon is 56 inches tall," Patty said. "When you know your height, record it on a Post-it in two ways. First, record it in inches, as you read it on the tape measure, and then in feet and inches. Patty wrote on the board:

56" or 56 in.

"You can write it in inches in either of these two ways," she said. "Then also record your height on the Post-it in feet and inches. How many feet are in 56 inches? Talk at your tables about that."

After a few moments, Patty asked for their ideas.

"It's 4 feet and 8 inches left over," Gina said. "We counted by 12s—12, 24, 36, 48, 60. We knew 60 was too much, so we went back to 48 and then counted up on our fingers to 56."

"I did it a different way," Leon said. "I know that 5 feet is 60 inches, so I knew that 56 inches is 4 inches less, so I took away 4 inches from 12 inches and got 8 inches. So it's 4 feet and 8 inches."

Patty recorded on the board:

4 ft. 8 in. or 4'8"

"You can write it either way," she said.

Patty then instructed the children to work together, measure their heights, record on Post-its, and post them on the board. When everyone was finished, the board was filled with 30 Post-its. Patty then asked the class a question.

"Who has an idea about how we could organize the Post-its so we can look at the information about everyone's height?" she asked. Hands flew up. Patty called on Alma.

"Put them in order from shortest to tallest," said Alma.

"If there are people with the same measurements, theirs should go in a column, one on top of the other," added Amon.

Patty quickly arranged the Post-its. As she did so, the students commented about the range of heights and noticed which measurements occurred more than once.

"Now that you have some experience measuring yourselves, how do you think scientists figured out that the blue whale can reach 100 feet in length?" Patty asked. "How do you think they measured a blue whale?"

"I think scuba divers measured some big ones and some little ones with underwater equipment," said Danica.

"They couldn't have measured them all because there are too many and they're hard to find," said Jésus.

"So you think they measured just a sample of whales?" Patty asked.

"Yes," several students answered.

"I think scientists measured some blue whales and then figured out how small and big they could get," said Tierney.

"If a scientist was using our measurements to report how tall a fourth grader might typically be, what might he or she say?" Patty asked.

"Between 4 and 5 feet," said Danica.

"About $4\frac{1}{2}$ feet tall because that's between 4 and 5 feet. It's kind of like an average," said Jill.

"I think a scientist would say that a fourth grader can reach 5 feet in height," said Gina.

"Here's what I'd like you to do now," said Patty. "Figure out about how many fourth graders would need to lie end to end to equal the length of a blue whale that's 100 feet long. You may use the data posted on the board to help you. Explain your thinking in words and numbers, and also include a picture, if you'd like."

The students worked on the problem until the end of the math period. Patty explained that they would continue their investigation during the following day's math period.

The Next Day

During math time the next day, the students resumed their work on the whale problem.

Amika, Danica, and Tierney added the heights of five students and arrived at a total of 21 feet 2 inches. Then they added the heights of six more students to come up with a measurement close to 100 feet. On her paper, Danica wrote: *Tierney, Amika, and I added inches and feet. We tryed to add short people and tall people. And we got 100' 5". I think it will take 20 people to equal 100 feet. But it took 21 people. I was really close.*

Alma's paper explained how her group used the repeat function on the calculator to help them solve the problem. She wrote: *We just put 51 and we pushed the plus button and the equal button and we got for an answer 1224 inches but we where sopos to get 1200 for an answer. But we got 1224 for an answer. . . . We think 24 4th graders would equal a blue whale because 51" × 24 = 1224" and a blue whal is 1200" long.*

Amon and Quimby used multiplication. Quimby wrote: *We rownded it off to 5 feet and times did 5 feet 20 times and came up with 100 feet. I chose 5 feet because it is easier then all of the other numbers. And some people are 5 feet tall.*

Amon and Quimby estimated 5 feet to be the average height of a fourth grader, then multiplied by 20 to get an answer.

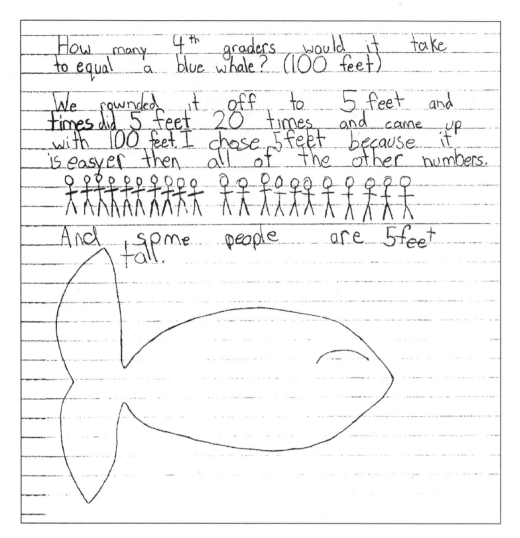

How many 4th graders would it take to equal a blue whale? (100 feet)

We rownded it off to 5 feet and times did 5 feet 20 times and came up with 100 feet. I chose 5feet because it is easyer then all of the other numbers.

And some people are 5feet tall.

Derek skip-counted by 5s to 100. He wrote: *One girl in my class is five feet and I counted by 5s and got 100 I think it would take 20 of her to eqal 100 feet. I pick 5 becase it was esey to count by fives.*

Jill solved the problem two different ways. She wrote: *20 people that are 5 feet tall each would fit in a blue whale. I chose 5 because its easy to count by and some kids are 5 feet tall. Inches—22 kids that are 56 inches tall would fit in a blue whale. I chose 56 because it was the mode and most people were 56 inches tall.*

Tanya and several other students chose 4 feet as the average height of a fourth grader. She wrote: *If you have 25 4th grade students that were each 4 ft. you would get 100 (the size of a blue whale). I chose 4 ft. because it is a factor of 100 and it's like counting quarters and because I realy like the number and its close to the average number in our class.*

Patty reported that this investigation was valuable for her students because it called for using several math skills, including estimating; adding; multiplying; measuring; and collecting, organizing, and using data.

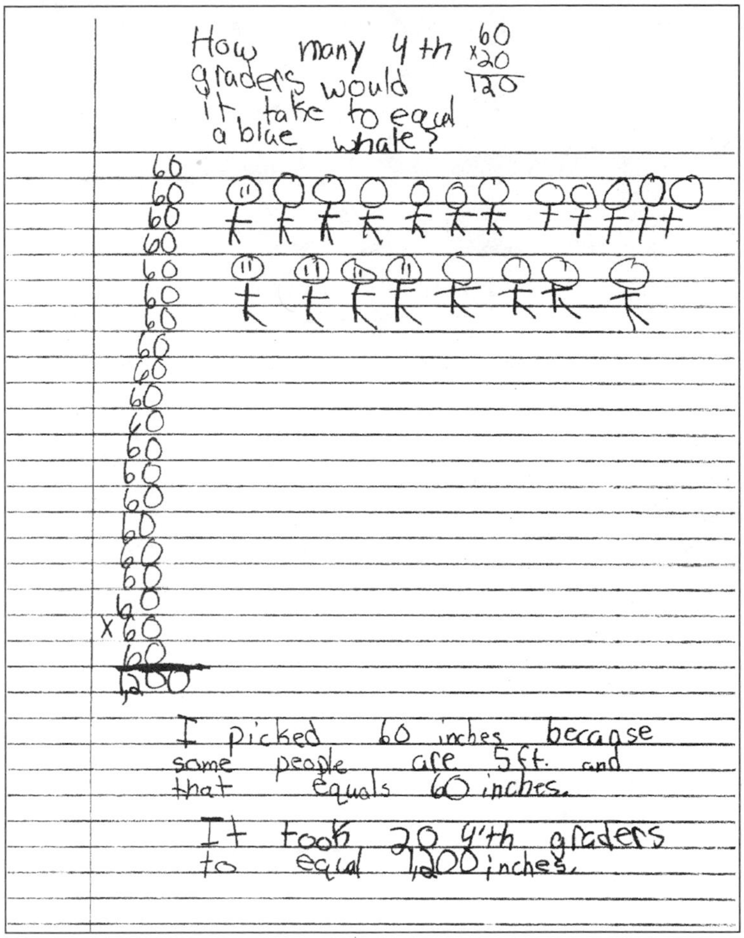

Handwritten student work:

> How many 4th graders would it take to equal a blue whale?
>
> $60 \times 20 = 120$ (shown as 60 × 20, 120)
>
> 60
> 60
> 60
> 60
> 60
> 60
> 60
> 60
> 60
> 60
> 60
> 60
> 60
> 60
> 60
> 60
> 60
> X 60
> 60
> 1200
>
> I picked 60 inches because some people are 5 ft. and that equals 60 inches.
>
> It took 20 4th graders to equal 1,200 inches.

Sawyer chose 60 inches as the average height and used repeated addition to solve the problem.

From a Fifth and Sixth Grade Class

I read the book to the fifth and sixth graders in my class. When I asked them how many of their lengths would equal the length of a blue whale, their estimates covered a wide range, similar to the estimates that Patty had reported from her fourth graders.

"I'm 6 feet tall," I told them. "How many feet would two of my lengths equal?"

"Twelve feet," the students chorused.

"How about four of my lengths?" I continued.

"Twenty-four feet," several students responded.

"How did you figure?" I asked.

"Because 6 feet times 4 of you would equal 24 feet," Tamar explained. "You use multiplication."

"How many of my lengths would equal 100 feet or the length of a blue whale?" I asked. Having them think about the relationship between my height and 100 feet helped them revise their estimates and make them more reasonable.

I then told the students that they were going to find out how many of their heights would equal the length of a blue whale. I had attached a tape measure to the wall in the back of the classroom, and I modeled for them how to measure height. I stood with my back to the tape and asked Jacob to hold a ruler on top of my head to see how tall I was.

"Work with a partner to find your height," I then said. "Also, draw a picture of yourself next to a blue whale. Your picture should show how your height compares to the length of the whale."

Since the students hadn't had much experience drawing pictures to scale, I asked them how they might approach doing this. I had them talk among themselves for a few minutes and then report their ideas to the class. The most popular idea suggested was that since a blue whale is about 100 feet long, they could draw a whale 10 inches long and say that each inch represented 10 feet.

Beverly rounded off her height to the nearest foot. She wrote: *I am four foot ten inches so twenty of my lengths would equal a blue whale. I got my answer by rounding four foot ten inches to 5 foot, and 5 × 20 is 100', a blue whales length.* She drew a picture of herself and her friend Heather next to the whale.

Beverly found the answer, then drew a proportional picture of herself and her friend Heather next to a whale.

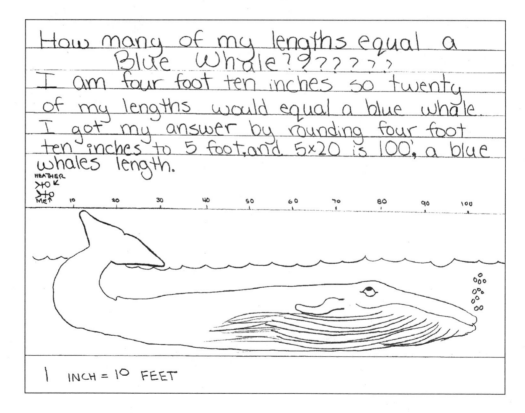

Brooke added and multiplied fractions to solve the problem. She wrote: *Because I'm 4 foot ½ and 4½ times 22 equals 99 and 99 is closer to 100. We added 4½ 22 times: 4 × 22 = 88 and ½ × 22 = 11 88 + 11 = 99.*

Bethia added fractions to find out how many of her lengths would equal the length of a blue whale. She wrote: *19 of my length would equal a blue whale. I'm 64 inches or 5 feet and 4 inches. or 5⅓ feet tall.* She kept adding 5⅓ until she got close to 100 feet. First she added 5⅓ 12 times, which equaled 64 feet. Then she added 5⅓ seven more times and got 37⅓ feet. Finally, she added 64 and 37⅓ together and got 101⅓ feet.

Bethia added fractions to solve the problem.

Some students measured desks and chairs and compared them with the blue whale's length. Shane and Jacob discovered in the school parking lot that about seven cars would equal the length of a blue whale.

Brittany converted the measurements to inches before tackling the problem. She wrote: *I multiplyed 100 × 12 because to see how big a blue whale can get in inches. I multiplyed 12 × 5 to see how tall I was in inches. I ÷ 1200 into 64 to see how many of me would fit the same size as a blue whale. It would take 18 Brittany's to reach the langth of a blue whale.*

Some children used division to solve the problem. Elias wrote: *I am 5 feet so I divided 5 into 100 and my answer is 20. I got the answer by dividing 5 into 100.* Elias drew a blue whale using a 1 inch = 10 feet scale. He and Leon then measured the length of the classroom and drew a picture of it next to the whale.

Jim and the Beanstalk

In *Jim and the Beanstalk*, by Raymond Briggs, Jim wakes up one day
to find a great plant growing outside his window. He decides to climb
up it into the clouds, where he finds a castle with an old, unhappy
giant. Unlike the original "Jack and the Beanstalk" tale, in this story
Jim helps the aging giant. When the giant complains about not being
able to see to read, Jim measures his huge head and returns to his
town to have giant eyeglasses made. Later, he measures the giant for
false teeth and a wig. The proportional illustrations help students as
they work to figure out the size of the giant's hand and then his height.

*materials·
tape measures or
rulers 1 per pr of students
3×3" sticky notes, 1 per student*

Caren Holtzman showed the cover of *Jim and the Beanstalk* to her sixth
graders. She asked the class, "By looking at the book's cover, do you have
any predictions or questions?"

"It's going to be like 'Jack and the Beanstalk,'" Patrick guessed.

"I think it will have something to do with measuring because of the picture on the cover," Martine added.

Caren began to read the book to her class. The students listened carefully as Jim went up the beanstalk to the giant's castle and back down again,
each time bringing the giant something new in return for gold. First, he
brought giant eyeglasses, then giant false teeth, and finally a giant wig. The
students' favorite part was the illustration showing Jim carrying a giant pair
of false teeth down the street, terrifying everyone in sight. The students
were amused by this updated version of the story and interested in Jim's
solutions to the giant's problems.

After she finished reading the book, Caren asked, "What did you think of
the story?"

"It's weird," said Tracy.

"Why?" asked Caren.

"It's totally different. The giant is supposed to eat him, but he didn't," Tracy
responded.

"In the other story, Jack stole from the giant," said Renee, "and in this story,
Jim gives stuff to the giant."

"How big do you think the giant is?" Caren asked the class. "Do you think
he could fit in our classroom?"

"He's about 50 feet tall," Otani said.

"Why do you think that?" asked Caren.

"Usually in stories the giant is 50 feet tall," he answered.

"I think he's really big because Jim is just the size of his ear," Tracy guessed.

"The giant coins look really big when Jim takes them," said Renee.

Caren showed the picture on the cover with Jim standing next to the giant's ear and then a page showing Jim next to one of the gold coins.

"So it sounds as if you're using two things to figure out the giant's size," Caren said. "You're using what you know from other stories, and you're using clues in this book. I'm going to ask you to think about the giant's hands. Could they fit in this room?"

"Both hands could fit," said Carson.

"What makes you think that?" asked Caren.

"We're the size of his ears, and his hands are about four times bigger, so they could both fit," Carson explained.

Caren held up the illustration that shows the giant sitting at his table, reading a little book. "On this page it looks as if the giant's thumb is about the size of the book," she said. "If his thumb is the size of a book, how long is his whole hand? What tools can you use to work on this problem?"

"A ruler or a measuring tape," said Audrey.

"It depends on the book," Carson added.

"Your job is to estimate the length of the giant's hand. You'll have to decide what size book to use for comparison. Then write your estimate on a Post-it and put it on the board. On lined paper, explain your thinking and tell how you got your answer. Any questions?"

"Can we work with partners?" Alejandro asked.

"Yes, you may work with a partner, but everyone needs to write a paper," Caren instructed. "One more thing. Since we'll be comparing our estimates, we need to decide on a unit of measure that we'll all use."

"Inches!" the students chorused.

The students found partners and searched for books to measure and rulers to measure them with. When they settled down, Caren circulated through the classroom and visited each table, asking questions and sometimes taking notes.

Ethan wrote: *We got three rulers and we mesured the book one time and we got $10\frac{1}{4}$ then we multiplied it by three. We multiplied the book because three tumbs make a hand. The answer is 30" $\frac{3}{4}$.*

Tracy and Audrey were working together. Audrey was measuring a book, while Tracy was measuring her hand in thumb-lengths. When they were finished, Tracy read from her paper: *"The giant's thumb is $7\frac{1}{2}$ inches and my hand is 7 inches. With my thumb next to my hand, it takes 3 of my sizes thumbs to make the size of my hand. So far the book that I am using, which is $7\frac{1}{2}$ inches, if you triple that it would be $22\frac{1}{2}$ inches. $7 \times 3 = 21 + 3$ halves is $22\frac{1}{2}$."*

"Why did you multiply the length of the book by 3?" Caren inquired.

"Because if our hands equal three of our thumbs, then we think the giant's hand equals three of his thumbs," explained Tracy. "We figured that $7\frac{1}{2}$ times 3 equals $22\frac{1}{2}$. So the giant's hand is $22\frac{1}{2}$ inches long."

Tracy explained how she multiplied the size of the book by 3 to determine the size of the giant's hand.

> The giant's thumb is 7½ inches and my round is 7 inches. With my thumb next to my hand, it takes 3 of my sizes thumbs to make the size of my hand. So far the book that I am using, which is 7½ inches, if you triple that it would be 22½ inches. 7×3=21 + 3 halves is 22½

Carey looked at the problem in two different ways. First he considered a book, his thumb, and the length and width of his hand. Then he took visual clues from the illustration on the book's front cover. He wrote: *The book is 9 inches long. My thumbe is 2 inches. My hand is six inches. My hand is 3× the size of my thumbe. My hand is 4 inches wide it is 2× the size of my thombe. So the with of his hand is 18 inches. By looking at the book the hand looks like it is 8 feet the kid looks like hes 4 feet long and the hand is 2× the size of the kid.*

"How do you know Jim is 4 feet tall?" asked Caren.

"Because I think that's the average height of a kid," Carey replied.

"Do you think everyone's hand measured across is two times the length of their thumb?" Caren asked.

"It seems like everyone at my table can go up their hand three times with their thumb. I think everyone could go across their hands two times with their thumbs, too, but I'm not sure," said Carey.

As the students completed their work, Caren reminded them to record their estimates on Post-its and to place them on the board in the front of the room. When everyone's estimate was posted, Caren asked the students for their attention.

"Can someone come up here and organize these Post-its so it's easier for us to look at the data?" she asked. Audrey volunteered and rearranged them into a horizontal line beginning with the lowest estimate and continuing to the highest.

Martine raised her hand. "I know something else we can do with them," she said. "Can I come up?" Caren nodded. Martine rearranged some of the Post-its, placing identical measurements in the same columns.

The Book is 9 inches long. my thumb is 3 inches. My hand is six inches. My hand is 2x the size of my thumb. My hand is 4 inches wide it is 2x the size of my thumb. So the with of his hard is 18 inches. By looking at the book the hand looks like it's 8 feet the Kid looks like he's 4 feet long and the hand is 2x the size of the kid.

the Kid

"Okay?" Caren asked Audrey. She nodded.

Caren then said, "Raise your hand if you can make a statement about the data." She called on Annika.

"Most think it's 30 inches," she said.

"What do you call the number that appears more often than any other?" asked Caren.

"The mode," several students answered in unison.

"The range is 22 inches to 48.75 inches," said Audrey.

"It depends on the book," Carson said.

"What do you mean?" asked Caren.

"If somebody has a book that's 9 inches, 9 times 3 equals 27, but if it's 10 inches, it's 10 times 3, and that's 30," he explained.

"It also depends on how big your hand is because my thumb is three times but someone else's may be four times up their hand," Janelle added.

"Let's test it," instructed Caren. "Everyone see how many thumbs long your hand is." The students quickly measured the lengths of their hands by using their thumbs. Many called out that their hands were three thumbs long. No one offered a different conclusion.

"Is it true for everyone?" asked Caren.

"Yes. If you have a bigger thumb, you have a bigger hand," said Mandy.

"Your thumb grows with your hand," Patrick said.

"I have three friends whose hands are $4\frac{1}{2}$ thumbs long," added Annika.

"So we're not certain that the length of everyone's hand measures three of their thumbs," Caren said, "but it seems like a typical measurement."

Caren then posed another question. "What's the average of the numbers we have up here?" she asked.

"Well, 30 is the mode and that's a kind of average," said Ethan.

"There's another way to find an average I learned last year, but I can't remember what it's called," said Tracy. She walked up to the board and removed from the graph the Post-it that read $22\frac{1}{2}$". She then went to the other end of the graph and removed 48.75". She continued to remove the Post-its from one end of the graph, then the other, until there was one Post-it left, which read 30".

"This is the number that's in the middle of the graph, and it's the average," said Tracy.

"Mathematicians call that kind of average the *median*," said Caren. "The median and the mode are the same in this case, but that's not always true."

Caren knew that her students were familiar with finding the mean as an average. She wanted them to see the benefits of looking at averages other than the mean, so she didn't pursue having them figure the mean. Too often, students think that the mean is the "real" way to determine an average.

Caren posed another question. "If the giant's hand is about 30 inches long, how tall is the giant?" Then she asked, "How might you figure this out?"

"You could find out how many hands tall you are and figure from there," said Martine.

"Measure yourself with your hand and use a calculator to multiply," suggested Dante.

"Measure yourself with your hand and multiply that by 30," said Joaquin.

"Look at the front cover picture for clues," said Carson.

"The cover picture has a tape measure next to the giant's head," said Audrey. "The inches on the tape look like feet instead of inches. You could use that to help you."

"So you think the scale is 1 inch equals 1 foot?" asked Caren.

"Yes," Audrey replied.

Caren wrote the three strategies on the board:

> *Use hand data.*
> *Use pictures from the book.*
> *Use the giant's head measurements.*

"I want each of you to commit to using a strategy for figuring the giant's height," she said. "Before starting on the problem, write your name on the board next to the strategy you plan to use." Students quickly signed up, gathered materials, and began to work.

Janelle used estimation to help her solve the problem. She wrote: *I think that the giant is 52 feet tall. Because one adult is like 5.2* [feet tall] *it looks in the book it could go like 10 times up. 5.2 × 10 = 52.*

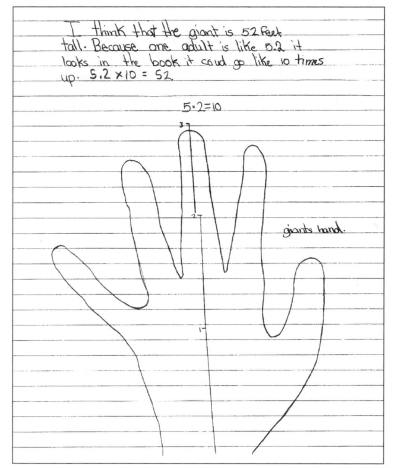

I think that the giant is 52 feet tall. Because one adult is like 5.2 it looks in the book it coud go like 10 times up. 5.2 × 10 = 52

5·2=10

giants hand.

Janelle estimated that an average adult is 5.2 feet tall, then multiplied by 10 to estimate the giant's height.

Joaquin and Patrick used the data from the giant's hand to solve the problem. Joaquin wrote: *You measure your Self with your hand and then times that with thirty because the giants hand is 30 inches and it is the same as me. I did that so it came up to 9 hands so I timesed 30 × 9 = 270. So the giant is 270 inches tall. So he is 22 and ½ feet tall. I know that because if you divide 12 ÷ by 270 on the calculator it will be 22.5. I divided those 2 numbers because 12" is one foot and 270 is how many inches he is.*

Otani and Nigel used a picture from the book to help them determine the scale. Otani wrote: *I think the giants is 32 feet tall. What I did is measured the boy and he was 1 inch tall. I think for every inch is 4 feet. So the boy is 1 inch so he's 4 feet now the giant is 8 inchs remember that 1 inch is 4 feet, so 8 × 4 = 32. What made me work this way is the picture on page 9. A normal kid is about 4 feet, so since he is a inch, that's why every 1 inch is 4 feet.*

Annika measured the length of the giant's head on the cover page. She used a 1" = 1' scale to determine the height of the giant. She wrote: *The giants head is nine feet so we think that your head can fit on your body about 10 times. So you do 10 times 9 will be 90 feet. So I think that the giant is about 90 feet.*

> # Giant's head (height)
> The head is 6 feet long, so then I measured how long my head on my body and I got 7 head from my head to my feet. So then I multiplied 6 by 7 and got 42 feet. So he is 42 feet tall.
>
> How I knew the giant's head was 6 feet long was if it was 6 inches long it wouldn't make sense but if it was six feet it would make sense.

After the students finished, Caren had them share their work by reading aloud what they had written. "What does this problem make you wonder about?" Caren asked.

"I'm wondering what the average height of a student in this room is," said Nigel.

"I'm still wondering if everyone's hand really is three of their thumbs tall," said Annika.

"Are we all 10 of our heads tall like Annika wrote?" asked Junipero.

"Is everyone's hand two of their thumbs wide?" asked Carson.

"When we say three thumbs equal a hand or 10 heads equal your height, we're talking about body ratios," Caren told the class.

"I wonder if there are other body ratios that are the same for everybody?" asked Bonita.

Caren felt that the students' final questions could be used as springboards for further investigations into scaling and measurement.

Reflecting on the experience, Caren commented, "This was an interesting activity because it dealt with the issues of measurement, ratio, and proportion. It was open-ended enough so the students could use many different strategies. Also, the way the students justified their thinking was important. Depending on which method or reference point in the book you used, 25 feet tall and 40 feet tall could both be correct answers."

Jumanji

In *Jumanji,* by Chris Van Allsburg, Peter and Judy find a board game in a nearby park and rush home to play it. By rolling dice and moving markers on the board, they make their way from the jungle to the city of Jumanji. Each time they land on a square that mentions a wild animal, that animal suddenly appears in the living room! The same thing happens with a monsoon and a volcanic eruption. The children are frightened, but at the end of the game, everything unusual disappears, and life returns to normal. The book provides a springboard to exploring probability with dice.

materials:
2 roll dice record sheet
1 per student
dice 1 pr per student

The sixth graders in Carol Schurlock's class listened with interest as I read the book *Jumanji*. The magical pastel drawings by the author fascinated the class. With the turn of each page, the students sat on the edge of their seats, anticipating the next disaster that would befall Peter and his sister Judy, the main characters in the story.

When I got to the part that reads, "Monsoon season begins, lose one turn," I stopped again, this time to ask a question.

"Raise your hand if you know what a monsoon is." Many hands shot up. I called on Claire.

"It's like a giant storm," she said. "I think it's tropical, too. We're studying about India and China right now, and we learned about monsoons."

When I read the part when the characters in the book are visited by a herd of stampeding rhinos, Blair exclaimed, "Wow! They'll get killed if they move!"

"Why's that, Blair?" I asked.

"Rhinos have poor eyesight, but they'll charge if they notice something moving," she explained. "There are Indian rhinos, and I think they're endangered."

I continued reading until I reached the part in the story where a volcano erupts in the house. I read, "'Molten lava poured from the fireplace opening. It hit the water on the floor and the room filled with steam.' Raise your hand if you know why the room filled with steam." I asked. I called on Gunther.

"Because when something hot hits cold water, it creates steam," he said.

I continued reading. "'If you roll a 12, you can get out of the jungle,' said Peter."

"Do you think it is likely or unlikely that Judy will roll a 12?" I asked. "Discuss this with someone next to you." After a few minutes, I repeated the question and called on Rowena.

"I think it is unlikely because there's only one way to make a 12 and that's to roll double 6s," she said.

"I think it's unlikely because there's only one 6 on each dice and the rest of the sides have other numbers on them," Silas said.

"I'm not sure because I think there's an equal chance to get any number," said Gunther.

"I think it's likely because I always see doubles rolled," Nico said.

"It's unlikely because there's a 1 out of 12 chance to get double 6s," explained Alexandra. "Because there's six numbers on each die and 6 plus 6 equals 12 and there's only one way to make 12 and that's 6 and 6."

As the students conjectured, I was thinking about how difficult it is to understand probability. Also, I knew that these students had limited experience with this area of mathematics.

When I finished reading the story, I said, "Let's go back to the page where Judy is hoping to roll a 12 to get out of the jungle." I quickly turned back to the page with the illustration of Judy sitting at a table, surrounded by rising steam.

"Judy wants to roll the sum of 12," I reminded the class. "What sum do you think she will most likely roll? Discuss this with the person next to you." When the discussion died down, I called on Lyric.

"I think that 8 is most likely to be rolled because you can get 8 in a few different ways, like 6 plus 2 and 5 plus 3 and 4 plus 4," she said.

"Seven is the most likely sum because you can get it by rolling a 5 and a 2, a 4 and a 3, and a 6 and a 1," said Seth.

"I think 10, but I'm not sure why," Raven added.

"Six is most likely because you can roll it a lot and, besides, it's between 2 and 12," said Deborah.

"Now that you've heard some people's reasons for choosing a 'most likely sum,' raise your hand if you think a sum of 2 is most likely to be rolled," I said. No one raised a hand. I continued to ask the class about the sums 2 to 12. Most students chose the sums 6, 7, and 8, a few chose 10, and two students thought that all of the sums had an equal chance of being rolled.

"We're going to do an activity called *Roll Two Dice*," I told the class. "The activity may help us find out which sums, if any, are more likely to be rolled than others."

I held up a recording sheet with the numbers 2 to 12 written along the top. Each number had its own vertical column with nine little squares. (See the next page and the blackline master on page 151.)

"Why do you suppose the recording sheet has the numbers 2 to 12?" I asked.

"Because those are the possible sums you can get when rolling the dice," said Blair.

"Can you get a sum of 13?" I asked.

"No!" they answered.

"Why not?" I asked.

Roll Two Dice

2	3	4	5	6	7	8	9	10	11	12

Finish Line →

"Because the numbers on the dice only go up to 6," Curt responded. "The largest sum you can get is 12, and 2 is the smallest."

"Here's how the game works," I began. "Each of you will receive a recording sheet and a pair of dice. Roll the dice, add the numbers together, and see what sum comes up. Find that sum on your recording sheet and write the addition sentence in the correct column. For example, if you rolled a 2 and a 4, you would write *2 + 4* below the 6. Keep rolling the dice and recording the addition sentences until the squares below one sum get to the finish line."

"What if we roll 5 and 2 and fill it in under the 7, and then we roll 5 and 2 again?" asked Alec. "Can we use a repeat?"

"Yes, that's okay," I replied. "Just record it again in the next space in the 7 column."

I then pointed to a large sheet of white butcher paper I had taped to the board. It had the numbers 2 to 12 written vertically down the left side.

"When you finish, record your data on this class chart," I said. "Bring your recording sheet up to the chart and make a tally mark for each time a sum came up. Let's say that the sum of 2 came up only twice. I would make two tally marks next to the 2 on our chart. If 9 came up on the dice four times, I would make four tally marks next to the 9 on our chart, and so on."

After I distributed the dice and the recording sheets, the students started playing Roll Two Dice. As they rolled the dice, they rooted for their favorite sums.

"Seven won again!" exclaimed several students throughout the activity.

"I finally rolled a 3!" someone shouted.

"Eight is winning!" Blair cried.

As the students recorded their data on the class chart, I gave additional recording sheets to those who wanted to do it again. When all the students had finished at least one sheet, I asked for their attention.

"Raise your hand if you'd like to make an observation about the data on our chart," I said. Many hands shot up. I called on Gabrielle.

"The winner is 7," she said.

"Two and 12 have the least number of tally marks because you can only roll them one way," Skye said. "You make a 12 with 6 plus 6 and a 2 with 1 plus 1."

"I see that 2 and 12 have about the same amount of tally marks," Silas said. "And 3 and 11 have about the same amount. It's the same for 4 and 10, 5 and 9, 6 and 8. And 7 has the most."

"So 7 is the mode," said Lyric.

"Lyric, explain what you mean by the mode," I said.

"It's the number that occurs the most," she explained.

"Eleven only has a few tally marks because there's only one way to make it," said Skye. "You can only make 11 by rolling a 6 and a 5."

"You could make it if you rolled a 5 and a 6," Blair said.

"That's the same thing!" Skye countered.

"I think there are two ways, 6 plus 5 and 5 plus 6, because the dice are different," argued Jarvis.

"You're just switching the positions of the dice, so it's the same thing," Augie responded.

"Some people think there's more than one way to make 11 and some think there's only one way," I said. "Discuss this with the people at your table so you can hear some other ideas." After about a minute, I asked for the students' attention.

"Raise your hand if you think 11 can be made only one way," I told them. About six hands went up.

"Who thinks 11 can be made in more than one way?" I asked. The rest of the class raised their hands. I decided to explain to the class why I thought the reversed addends counted as different ways. I held up one red die and one green one and pointed out that getting a 6 on the red and a 5 on the green was different from getting a 6 on the green and a 5 on the red one.

"I still think it's the same thing," said Augie. A few students nodded their agreement. I wanted the students to examine their reasoning, so I asked more questions.

"How many ways are there to make 7?" I asked.

"There are six ways," said Lyric. "3 plus 4, 4 plus 3, 5 plus 2, 2 plus 5, 6 plus 1, and 1 plus 6." I wrote these addition combinations on the board.

"I think there are only three ways," said Augie. "3 plus 4, 5 plus 2, and 6 plus 1." I circled these addition combinations as a way of showing Augie's opinion.

"What about 8?" I asked. "How many ways for 8?" I called on Jarvis.

"There are five ways: 2 plus 6 and 6 plus 2, 5 plus 3 and 3 plus 5, and 4 plus 4," he said. Again, I recorded the addition combinations on the board.

"I disagree," said Nico. "There's only three ways to get an 8: 4 plus 4, 6 plus 2, and 5 plus 3."

"Here's my question," I said. "If what Augie and Nico are saying is true and there are the same number of ways to make 7 and 8, then why are there so many more tally marks on 7?"

"Because 7 is a middle number on the graph, and you can roll it more often," said Jarvis.

"Yes, 7 is in the middle but it has more tally marks because there are more ways to make that number!" exclaimed Blair.

While most of the students in the class understood, for example, that 3 + 4 and 4 + 3 are two different possibilities, there were still some students who were not convinced. They were holding firm to their beliefs, and I knew that teaching by telling was not going to work. It often takes time and experience for students to make sense of a new idea.

"Let's go back to the question I asked you to think about earlier," I said. "When rolling the dice, what sum do you think is most likely to be rolled? I want each of you to write a convincing argument that explains and justifies your thinking."

The students' writing revealed a range of thinking about probability. I visited each table, asking the children questions and listening to their ideas.

Marius wrote: *I think when rolling 2 dice its more likely to roll a 7 because it's in the middle and there's 6 ways to roll it. Even though 6 and 8 are in the middle and have 5 ways, 7 has more numbers possible to roll and is closer to the middle than eight. Plus it is in between 6–8.*

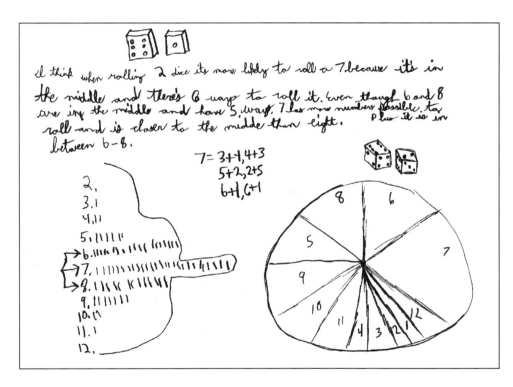

Marius reproduced the class chart and drew a pie graph to show that 7 was the most likely number.

Blair wrote: *When rolling the dice, I think 8 is the number to come up most likely because you can get 8 by rolling: 2 + 6, 6 + 2, 3 + 5, 5 + 3, and 4 + 4. there are 5 ways to get an 8.*

After Blair read her paper to me, I said to her, "Blair, during our class discussion you said that there are more tally marks next to the 7 because there are more ways to make it. I'm curious to know why you're choosing 8 now."

"I think 8 because there's not that many more ways to make 7 than 8," she answered. "They're pretty close. Seven won't always happen."

Jarvis wrote: *I think that the 7 would come up most, because where it's position is and if you look at the graph it lowers and in the middle it gets bigger than lowers and it has 6 ways to get it, 3 + 4, 4 + 3, 5 + 2, 2 + 5, 6 + 1, 1 + 6.*

Jarvis argued that 7 would come up most.

There were some students who realized that there were more ways to make 6, 7, and 8, but held the belief that there was an equal chance that any number could be rolled. For example, Gunther wrote: *When I roll two dice I think all of the numbers have a 50 50 of geting rolled on because we can't control the way the dice rolls. The dice rolls were ever it wants and no one can make it roll were ever he/she wants. Sure other numbers have more ways to get it, but on one dice you can only get 1, 2, 3, 4, 5, or 6. And on the other dice you can roll the same numbers. So it's a 50 50 chance of geting any number.*

After the students completed their writing, several volunteered to read aloud what they had written. This helped the other students reflect and clarify their thinking about the mathematical situation they had just encountered. Everyone except Gunther agreed that some sums are more likely to come up than others. However, there wasn't a consensus about how many ways each sum could be made, and my goal wasn't to push everyone to agree. Some students needed further experiences and more time to think about the possible outcomes when two dice are rolled. At this time, I wanted the students to explore the idea that some events are more likely to occur than others and why and to have experience predicting outcomes and collecting and analyzing data.

The King's Chessboard

> *The King's Chessboard,* by David Birch, tells the story of a king who insists on giving a gift to his wise man. The man wants no gift but finally points to a chessboard and suggests that the king give him one grain of rice for the first square of the chessboard and on subsequent days double the amount of the previous day's unit until all 64 squares of the chessboard are covered. Not understanding how much rice would be needed, the king agrees. After 31 days, he realizes that he can't fulfill his agreement. The book leads into a lesson in which children use multiplication and measurement. Note: *The Rajah's Rice: A Mathematical Folktale from India,* by David Barry, and *A Grain of Rice,* by Helena Clare Pittman, offer similar stories that can also be springboards for this lesson. (See the Bibliography on page 153.)

Materials:
zip-top bags of rice
1 per group of 3–4 students
plastic teaspoons 1 per group of 3–4
measuring cups 1 per group

"**I** have a book I want to share with you called *The King's Chessboard,*" I told Patti Reynolds's fifth and sixth graders. "It's a story that's set in India a long time ago."

I began reading the story. The children enjoyed the pen and watercolor illustrations by Devis Grebu. Many students commented on the curved domes and elegant archways of old India. I stopped after I read the part where the wise man proposes rice as a reward for his good services.

"In the story, the wise man asks to receive 1 grain of rice on the first day, then 2 grains on the second day, then 4, 8, 16, and so on," I said. I recorded on the board:

1, 2, 4, 8, 16

"There were 64 squares on the king's chessboard," I continued. "What's happening to the number of grains each day?"

"They're doubling," several students chorused.

"You multiply the number by 2 to get the next number on the chessboard, like 1 times 2 equals 2, then 2 times 2 equals 4, and 4 times 2 equals 8," explained Rachel.

"I want you to think about how many grains of rice will be delivered on the 64th day," I instructed. "You may discuss this with the people at your table, but I want you each to write your own answer and explain how you got it."

"Do we have to come up with an exact answer?" Jackson asked.

"No, an estimate will do," I responded. "But you'll need to explain why your answer makes sense."

It was difficult for the students to estimate. Most jotted down a guess, then proceeded to dive into the problem with their calculators in hand.

As I walked from table to table, I noticed that many students were drawing pictures of chessboards and writing the numbers of grains in each square. After about 10 minutes, I began to hear exclamations of surprise from several groups.

"The numbers are getting huge!" Everett cried.

"The display on my calculator won't fit the numbers anymore!" exclaimed Caitlin.

One group of students was gathered around Emanuel, who had a calculator that could display larger numbers. While Emanuel pressed the buttons on his calculator, another group member read the number on the display, and a third student recorded the number on paper.

After about 20 minutes, I began a class discussion.

"Raise your hand if you'd like to report your answer and what you did," I said. I called on Meredith.

"I think there will be about 500 billion grains of rice on the 64th day," she said. "First I drew a picture of a chessboard and then I doubled each number. On the 22nd day, there would be 2,097,152 grains of rice. I figured that if there was that many on the 22nd day, the number of grains on the 64th day would be really big."

Jackson read from his paper, "*I started at one and kept timesing it on the calculator and each time I times it I make a slash and I've gotten to 20 slashes and that's about $\frac{1}{3}$ of the way and I have 529,288 already. So I take the other 20 squares and that makes 40 squares so I times that by two and that makes 80. I'm going to times my answer by 80 and that's my guess and that's 42,343,040 grains of rice.*"

"*I think that it will be 10,819,476,736 grains of rice,*" said Lexie, reading the number from her paper. She then explained, "If you double the numbers up to the 32nd square, you multiply that number by 32 because you need 32 more to get 64 squares."

"My estimate is 128 because 64 squares is half of that and 64 times 2 equals 128," said Reed. Although some students looked surprised when they heard Reed's estimate, they were respectful and listened to his reasoning.

Only a few students made estimates in the range of the one Reed made. Most students realized that, with doubling, the number of grains grew very fast. After their calculators became useless, many students began to multiply but some just guessed.

When all the students who were interested in sharing their results had done so, I continued with the story. The students were amazed at the amount of rice the king had to give the wise man.

"Is there a lesson to be learned in this story?" I asked. I called on Ursula.

"The lesson is, go to school!" she exclaimed. Everyone laughed.

"I think the lesson is that if you let pride get in the way, you're in for trouble," said Corinne.

The Kings Chestboard!
(Estimation)

1 day—1
2 day—2
3 day—4
4 day—8
5 day—16
6 day—32
7 day—64
8 day—128
9 day—256
10 day—512
11 day—1024
12 day—2048
13 day—4096
14 day—8192
15 day—16384
16 day—32768
17 day—65536
18 day—131072
19 day—262144
20 day—524288
21 day—1048576
22 day—2097152
23 day—4194304
24 day—8388608
25 day—16777216
26 day—33554432
27 day—67108864
28 day—1342177728
29 day—2684354556
30 day—536870912
31 day—1073741824
32 day—2147483648

I think that it will be
108194476736 grains of Rice.
Because if double number
till 32 and you multiply by 32
because you need 32 more. You
will get that number.

$$67108864$$
$$\times 2$$
$$134217728$$

$$1+$$
$$268435456$$
$$\times 2$$

$$+$$
$$536870912$$
$$\times 2$$

$$+$$
$$1073741824$$
$$\times 2$$

$$2147483648$$
$$\times 32$$
$$4294967296$$
$$+6524589440$$
$$108194476736$$

"I have another mathematical question for you to solve," I then said. "On which square would enough rice arrive to feed everyone in the class? Talk about this with the people at your table. What do you need to know in order to solve this problem?" After a minute or so, several hands were raised. I called on Ray.

"We need to know how many kids and adults are in our room," he said. We quickly counted that there were 33 people, and I wrote on the board:

33 people

"We also need to know how much rice each person will eat," said Annie. I told them that ½ cup was a standard serving size, and I wrote on the board:

½ cup per person

"Then we need to know how many grains of rice are in a half cup," said Garrett. "I think it will take a long time to count the grains in a half cup."

"Can anyone suggest an easier way to find out how many grains of rice there are in ½ cup?" I asked.

"Why don't we find out how many teaspoons of rice there are in ½ cup and count the grains in one teaspoon, and go from there?" suggested Caitlin. We agreed to try that method.

Several students helped me pass out a baggie of rice, plastic spoons, and a measuring cup to each group.

"Work together to find out how many level teaspoons of rice are in ½ cup," I instructed. The groups quickly worked this out, and students were soon flapping their hands in the air, eager to share their answers. I called on one group at a time and wrote all of their answers on the board:

Teaspoons: 26 30 33 29 30 21 33 32

"We have a range of 21 to 33 teaspoons," I observed. "Raise your hand if you can explain why we have so many different answers?"

"Maybe the rice was not completely level in each teaspoon," said Dale.

"Some people were less precise than others," Annie said.

"The measuring cups are different and some are confusing to read," added Moss.

"How can we decide on one number for all of us to use to solve the problem?" I asked.

"Let's find out the average," Emanuel suggested.

"Raise your hand if you can explain a way to find the average," I said. I called on Keith.

"You add all of the numbers together and divide by 8 because 8 is how many numbers there are," Keith said.

The students quickly took out calculators and did what Keith suggested. They figured the average, got 29.25 and decided to use 29. I wrote *29 teaspoons* on the board. I knew that this wasn't an accurate measure of how many teaspoons are in ½ cup (there are 24), but since all of the students' measurements would be approximate, I decided to go with this number.

"Now I want each group to figure out how many grains of rice are in a teaspoon," I instructed.

The groups worked together in a variety of ways. In two groups, the members each counted their own teaspoons of rice, then calculated the average. Two groups grouped the grains in 10s to count. In some groups, everyone helped to count; in others, only one person counted while the rest kept track of the numbers. When they finished, I recorded each group's result:

170 grains
160
212
195
278
330
265
212

The students calculated the average to be 227.75, and decided to round it to 228 grains of rice in a teaspoon.

"How can we figure out how many grains of rice are in ½ cup?" I asked. "Discuss this with your group." After a few minutes, I repeated the question and called on Kelsey.

"There are 29 teaspoons of rice in ½ cup and 228 grains of rice in a teaspoon, so you multiply 228 times 29," she explained.

"Is there another way?" I asked. No one raised a hand. The students quickly used their calculators to determine that in ½ cup there would be 6,612 grains of rice.

"Because our measurements aren't really exact, our answer is an approximation. But a number like 6,612 seems to imply that we know exactly how many grains of rice. Raise your hand if you can think of a number we can use that is a reasonable approximation for 6,612." I said. Nearly everyone's hand shot up in the air.

"I think you should round it up to 7,000," Ursula suggested.

"Maybe 6,600," Ray said.

"Or 6,500," Corinne added.

"What number should we use?" I asked. "All of these are possible."

"I think 7,000," Lexie said. "All of our measurements were different, and this seems easy to understand." There was unanimous agreement from the class.

"I have a question," Rachel said. "Is ½ cup of cooked rice the same as ½ cup of uncooked rice?"

Rachel's question was not a surprise to me. Earlier in the lesson, I had told the students that ½ cup of rice was a standard serving. I didn't specify whether this was cooked or uncooked. I decided to wait and see if someone would inquire about this. Had Rachel not asked this important question, I would have raised it with the group.

"Rice generally expands to three times its original uncooked size," I said. "Discuss this with your group and see if this changes how we should approach our problem."

When at least one hand was raised in each group, I had students report.

"I think that you need to multiply 7,000 by 3 because there needs to be more rice," said Noreen.

"I disagree," Sid said. "You need to divide by 3 because the rice gets bigger so you don't need as much." A flurry of comments erupted as students gave support to Noreen's or Sid's idea. I called the students to attention.

"Thumbs up if you think we should multiply by 3 and thumbs down if you think we should divide by 3," I said. Most of the students thought that dividing was the correct operation to use. I asked them to take a few minutes in their groups to discuss this. "Try and make a convincing argument for your position," I said.

When the discussions died down, the issue was resolved. The students agreed to divide. The students calculated that 7,000 divided by 3 was about 2,333 grains per ½ cup.

"So, the problem is to figure out how many grains of rice it would take to feed all of us," I said. "I also want you to find out on what square there would be enough rice to feed us. You may discuss the problem with your group members, but you are each responsible for your own paper."

The class seemed to take this last question very seriously and worked quietly for more than 30 minutes. When they were finished, I asked for their attention.

Esme explained why enough rice to feed the class would arrive on the 18th day.

"Raise your hand if you'd like to share your answer and explain your thinking," I said. I called on volunteers to read their papers aloud.

Jackson read: *"Each person gets 2,333 grains of rice so I figured out how much rice the class needs to feed everybody by takeing how much one person gets and times it by how many people their are in the class and that's 33 so I did this: 2,333 × 33 = 76,989. And Im going to I figur out what day they would bring about how much rice it takes to feed the class by starting at one and times by two up to the anser puting a slash each time. 131,072 grains of rice will arive on the 18 day."*

Noreen read: *"The whole class will get 131,072 grains of rice. They will get it on the 18th day. How I got this answer is I looked at the chart we used for The King's Chessboard."*

Ray read: *"We will need 76,989 to feed 33 people. We will reach or get that amount in the 17 day will be to little, But in the 18th it will be to much so it's 17½ days. We will have enough rice at the 17th day at 6:00 pm."*

Liv figured that there would be enough rice on the 17½ day.

When students finished sharing their work, I held up another book, called *The Rajah's Rice: A Mathematical Folktale from India,* by David Barry.

"This book is very similar to *The King's Chessboard*," I told them. "At the back of the book, there's an illustration of a chessboard with 64 squares. In each square there is a drawing and a number explaining how many grains of rice arrive. For example, on the 32nd square, enough rice would arrive to fill 256 wheelbarrows. On the 64th square, there would be a stack of rice as large as Mount Kilimanjaro!"

This elicited exclamations of surprise from the students. Esme asked, "How big is Mount Kilimanjaro?"

"I don't know," I answered.

Sid rushed to the bookshelf. He opened a book about geography to a page showing Mount Kilimanjaro compared to the other big mountains of the world.

"Mount Kilimanjaro is 19,340 feet high, and it's the fourth tallest mountain in the world!" he exclaimed. "That would be a lot of rice!"

A Million Fish . . .
More or Less

Strange things happen on the Bayou Clapateaux, or so Hugh Thomas learns in *A Million Fish . . . More or Less,* by Patricia C. McKissack. He catches three small fish—and then a million more. But before he can get all those fish home, Hugh meets an alligator, which demands a half share; raccoon bandits, which take half of the remaining share; and a hungry cat, which takes more than its share. Hugh arrives home with just enough fish for dinner—three small ones. The story leads to a discussion of large numbers and an activity in which children assign numbers to various objects and events.

materials: none

I read *A Million Fish . . . More or Less* to Dinah Brown's fourth graders near the beginning of the school year. The class had been investigating large numbers, and Dinah's goal was for her students to improve their number sense.

"Have any of you ever exaggerated when you told someone about something?" I asked. Whispers broke out across the room, mixed with a few giggles.

"I remember one time that I told my friends that my dad got a Cadillac, and I said that it was 100 feet long!" said Grant.

"That would be pretty long for a car," I said. "Was that how long it really was?" I asked.

"No," Grant said. "It really was only about, say, 15 feet long, but I wanted to impress my friends."

"Has anyone else exaggerated before?" I asked.

"One time I went fishing with my dad, and I caught a fish, and I told my mom that it weighed over a hundred pounds," said Ned. "It really only weighed about a couple of pounds."

"I have a story I want to read to you about a boy who catches a million fish—more or less," I told them. "The setting of the story is a swamp. Raise your hand if you know what a swamp is." Lots of hands went up.

"It's a place that's really muddy," offered Tama.

"I think weird animals live in them, like alligators and stuff like that," Nadine guessed.

"It's a place where there's water, like a river or a lake," said Anton.

"You seem to know a lot about swamps," I commented. "This story is about Hugh Thomas, a boy who goes fishing in a river near a swamp."

I began to read the book. The children's imaginations were captured by both the story and Dena Schutzer's beautiful illustrations. They laughed when I read the part in the book where the two swampers, Elder Abbajon and Papa-Daddy, tell Hugh Thomas a whopper of a story about a turkey: "Take the time back in '03, me and the Elder here caught a wild turkey weighed five hundred pounds!"

The children snickered in disbelief when Papa-Daddy, lowering his voice to a whisper, told the story of the lantern: "As we was marchin' that gobbler home, I spied a lantern that'd been left by Spanish conquistadores back in the year 15 and 42. And it was still burning!"

"Could a turkey really weigh 500 pounds?" I asked.

"No!" chorused the class.

"Could a lantern really burn for 350 years?" I asked. (The correct length of time is 450 years, but the characters in the book say 350.)

"No!" the students answered back.

I continued to read the story, stopping at the part where Hugh Thomas meets Atoo, "the *grand-père* of all the alligators" in the swamp. At this point in the story, Hugh Thomas had his million fish loaded on his little red wagon.

Atoo slithered onto the bank and, blocking Hugh Thomas, demanded some of the catch. The boy decided not to tangle with Atoo, and threw about half of his catch back into the bayou.

"If Hugh Thomas really had a million fish, and threw half of them back for Atoo, how many fish would Hugh Thomas be left with?" I asked. "Talk with the people in your group and try to figure this out."

After a few minutes, I asked the students for their attention and repeated the question.

"I think Hugh Thomas would have 5,000 fish left," said Jillian.

"I think it would be 50,000 fish left," said Colette.

"He would have half a million," Drew said.

"I think he would have 500,000 fish when he left Atoo," Tama added.

Most of the children weren't sure how many fish were half of a million. I decided that taking halves of powers of 10 might help them think about the question. I began by writing the number *10* on the board.

"What's half of 10?" I asked.

"Five," they responded. I recorded a *5* next to the *10.*

Then I wrote *100* under the *10.* "What's half of 100?" I asked.

"Fifty," they answered. I recorded *50* next to the *100.*

Then I wrote *1,000* under the number *100,* and asked the class, "Do you know what half of 1,000 is?"

"Five hundred," they answered.

"So all of these were pretty easy for you," I said. "But what if someone weren't sure about your answers. How could you prove, for example, that 500 is half of 1,000?" Many students raised their hands. I called on Drew.

"It's simple," he said. "Just add 500 and 500, and you get 1,000, so it's half."

"I know another way," Lizette said. "You can go 2 times 500 is 1,000."

I then wrote *10,000* under the *1,000*. "Let's read this together," I said. After the students read 10,000 aloud, I asked them to figure out half of 10,000. I called on Amber.

"It's 5,000. All the answers have 5s and zeros," she observed.

"And there's one more zero each time," Matthias added.

Next I wrote *100,000*. "Who can read this number?" I asked. About half of the students raised their hands.

"Let's say it together," I said. I had the students read the number again so those who hadn't been sure could join in.

"What's half of 100,000?" I asked. Again, about half of the students raised their hands. I called on Ned.

"Half of 100,000 is 50,000," he said.

"How did you figure?" I asked.

"I just kept going," Ned answered. "It had to be a 5 with four zeros."

"How else could you explain that 50,000 is half of 100,000?" I asked. I waited a few moments until about eight hands were raised. I called on Simone.

"I know 50 is half of 100. So it makes sense that 50,000 is half of 100,000," Simone emphasized the "thousand" each time in her explanation.

Ernest raised his hand. "It's right," he said. "I did it on the calculator, and I got the same thing."

"Now for the big one," I told the class. I wrote *1,000,000* on the board.

"This is the number of fish Hugh Thomas said he had before he gave Atoo half of his catch," I said. Some of the students murmured "one million."

"Can you use the pattern on the board to figure out what is half of 1,000,000?" I asked.

"I know how to write it," said Lizette. Lizette wrote the number *500,000* on the board, and we all read it together. Ernest verified the answer on the calculator.

"Could you prove this is correct the way you proved that 500 was half of 1,000?" I asked Drew.

"Sure," he said. Drew came to the board, wrote two 500,000s, one underneath the other, and added them to get 1,000,000.

I continued reading the story. Hugh Thomas followed the swamp path to Papa-Daddy and Elder Abbajon's houseboat. The children listened closely as I read about ghosts and pirates' treasure. The students' anticipation rose when I read: "The boy hummed and quickened his step. Something was stalking him, closing in fast."

"What do you think was stalking him?" I asked.

"A snake?" Kristy guessed.

"A raccoon!" Lizette said confidently.

"You seem very sure of yourself," I said, half joking.

"There was a picture of a raccoon on the cover of the book," Lizette said.

"Sure enough," I responded. "A raccoon named Mosley stopped Hugh Thomas and demanded a toll. The boy offered him half of his catch."

I stopped reading and asked the class, "If Hugh Thomas had 500,000 fish and Mosley the raccoon took half, how much would Hugh Thomas have? Talk to the people at your table to figure it out." When the children's voices died down, I asked for their ideas.

"Half of 500,000 is 50,000," said Ernest.

"I think it's 300,000, because 3 is in the middle of 100,000 and 500,000," Barbara said.

"You can't get one half of 500,000 because 5 is an odd number and you can't split it evenly," said Justine.

"What's half of 5?" I asked.

"Two and a half," answered Anton.

"Sometimes mathematicians write $2\frac{1}{2}$ as 2.5," I explained. "I'm going to record some numbers on the board again and see if you can figure out half of 500,000 by looking at a pattern."

To begin the pattern, I wrote *5* and recorded half of it as 2.5. I then wrote *50,* and the students readily offered 25. I continued with 500, 5,000, 50,000, and finally 500,000, each time asking how much was half and recording the answer. While some students seemed to have a sense of half of each quantity, others figured by following the emerging number pattern.

5	*2.5*
50	*25*
500	*250*
5,000	*2,500*
50,000	*25,000*
500,000	*250,000*

I returned to the book. Mosley wouldn't settle for only half of Hugh Thomas's catch; he demanded it all. Hugh Thomas suggested a contest. Mosley agreed to a jump-rope (actually, a jump-snake) contest. If Mosley jumped more times, he would get all of Hugh Thomas's catch; if Hugh Thomas jumped more times, then he would give the raccoon only half of the catch. Mosley jumped 5,552 times before missing, but Hugh Thomas won by making 5,553 jumps.

"Do you think it's likely that they jumped that many times?" I asked.

"No!" the children responded.

I then said, "Maybe 5,000 couldn't be the number of times a person jumps rope, but it could be . . ." I left the last part of my sentence for the students to complete.

"The number of pounds an elephant weighs!" answered Simone.

"The amount of money in a savings account!" added Elliott.

I finished reading the book, and then I turned back to the part where the two swampers were telling the story about the turkey and the lantern.

"Remember when the swampers said that the turkey weighed 500 pounds?" I asked. The students nodded.

"Five hundred couldn't be the number of pounds a turkey weighs, but it could be . . . ," I said, again leaving the sentence unfinished for the students.

"It could be the number of students in our school," said Ben.

I continued, "And 350 couldn't be the number of years a lantern could stay lit, but it could be . . ." Many hands shot up this time.

"The number of days in almost a year!" Keziah said, giggling. The class laughed with her.

I then wrote on the board:

_____ *could not be the number of* _____,
but it could be the number of _____.

"Suggest some numbers that we could use to begin the sentence," I said.

The students offered many numbers. Their suggestions ranged from 3 to 1,000,000. After recording about 20 numbers on the board, I explained what they were to do.

"Pick a number, either one from the board or any other you'd like to use," I instructed. "Use the number to begin the sentence I wrote on the board, then complete the sentence and illustrate what you wrote."

"Can we do more than one number?" Colette asked.

"Yes," I said. "You should do two numbers, and then we'll put all of your work together into a class book. One of the numbers you choose should be a large number, and one of the numbers should be a small number. Then, if you'd like, you can do another page."

"What's a large number and what's a small number?" asked Nadine.

"That depends on how you think about it," I said. "A number that is small in one situation can be large in another."

"What do you mean?" Ned asked.

"If I said that I saw a person eat eight apples, that's a large number of apples for someone to eat," I explained. "But if I said that a total of eight people attended a rock concert, that would be a very small audience. In the first situation, 8 is a large number; in the second, it's tiny."

The children got to work. As I walked around the room, I listened to them talk with their neighbors about the numbers they chose. Also, I asked some children questions about what they were writing.

Matthias was writing down his thoughts about 1,000,000. I asked him to read to me what he wrote. He read: *"1,000,000 could not be the number of a person's age, but it could be the number of people in Mexico."*

"You're right, Matthias, that a person can't be 1,000,000 years old," I said. "But I once visited a Mexican city that had a population of about 1 million, so I know the population of the whole country of Mexico is much greater. I think you need to do some research about the population of Mexico. Where could you find that information?"

"In our social studies book," he replied, and he hurried over to the bookshelf to begin his research.

Kristy chose a number with which she was comfortable. She wrote: *50 could not be the number of stripes on the flag, but it could be the number of stars on the flag.*

30 could not be the number of kids or people in a school but it could be the number of kids in a class

Tyler was struggling with the number 9,999. He was able to identify what the number could not be (he chose a person's age), but he was stumped when it came to thinking of something that numbered 9,999. Marnie, who was sitting next to him, offered some help.

"When I was in northern California, we visited the redwood trees. I think that some redwoods are about 10,000 years old," she said.

Maureen wrote: *25 could not be the number of hairs on your head, but it could be the number of books you read in a month.*

"Is it possible for someone to have 25 hairs on their head?" I asked.

"If you're my father," she said, without cracking a smile.

Lizette was having fun with her paper. She wrote: *1,000,000 could not be the number of socks you have, but it could be the number of socks in the world. What a disgusting odor!*

When the students finished writing, I had volunteers share their work with the rest of the class. Some of what students wrote was immediately called into question by the others, giving the students a chance to teach one another about numbers. For example, when Lizette shared her thoughts about 1,000,000 being the number of socks in the world, Matthias raised his hand.

"When I was looking at our social studies book, I found out that there are over 3 billion people on Earth," he said. "So I don't think that there would only be 1,000,000 socks in the world."

"How many pairs of socks do you think each person would have?" I asked.

"I have about six pairs," said Lizette.

"What if each person in the world had as many pairs of socks as Lizette. How many socks would that be?" I asked. "Talk with the people at your table and see what you come up with." After a minute or so, several hands were raised. I called on Ben.

"I liked Lizette's idea, because my paper had to do with the number of people in the world, too," he said. "We think that if you have 6 pairs of socks, that's 12 socks. Then you would have to multiply 12 times 3 billion and $12 \times 3 = 36$. So that would be 36 billion socks!"

Lizette's idea about the number of socks in the world was called into question.

1,000,000 could not be the number of socks you have, but it could be the number of socks in the WORLD (what a disgusting odor!)

When Douglas shared his idea that 500,000,000 could not be the number of whales in Sea World, but it could be the number of people in the United States, Artrina disagreed.

"I don't think there are that many people in the U.S.," she said.

"I know there are; I read it in a book," Douglas countered.

I tabled the disagreement by writing Douglas's idea on the board under the title "Under Investigation."

Simone's writing led to an entirely new investigation. She read from her paper: *"60 couldn't be the number of people in the world, but it could be the weight of a fourth grader."*

"Get out the scale," Grant responded.

One good lesson often leads to another, and in this case, the students led the way.

Mr. Griggs' Work

> *Mr. Griggs' Work*, by Cybil Rylant, tells the story of a post office employee who loves his work. Mr. Griggs has spent many years working at the local post office. He likes his work so much that he "thought about it almost all the time." Even when not at work, he thinks about where lost packages might have ended up, how much it might cost to mail a package to New Zealand or a 3-ounce letter to Taiwan, and how chipmunks remind him of a stamp issued in 1978. This 13-cent chipmunk stamp provides a springboard to a lesson in which students look for patterns in postal rate increases since 1917 and predict what it will cost to mail a 1-ounce letter in the year 2005.

"Is there a post office near your school?" I asked Patti Reynolds's fifth and sixth graders to begin the lesson.

"Yes!" the students chorused.

"It's just down the hill," Spencer added.

"I have a book I'd like to share with you that's about a man who works at a post office," I said. "His name is Mr. Griggs, and he really loves his job."

I began reading *Mr. Griggs' Work* to the class. The students were surprised that anyone could love work as much as Mr. Griggs did. They thought it was funny that he was so preoccupied by letters and packages and stamps. After I read that Mr. Griggs wondered how much it would cost to mail a package to New Zealand or a letter to Taiwan, I asked the students a question.

"Has anyone mailed a letter to a place far away?" I asked. Several hands went up. I called on Reed.

"I've mailed letters to England and Germany, and I think I had to put three stamps on them," he said.

"I sent one to France, but I can't remember how much it cost," said Jackson.

"How much does it cost to mail a letter in the United States?" I asked .

"Thirty-two cents," the students chorused.

When I finished reading the book, I went back to the page that has a picture of Mr. Griggs sitting on the ground having a picnic.

"This picture shows Mr. Griggs looking at the chipmunk stamp of 1978," I said. "The price on the stamp is 13 cents. That's how much it cost to mail a 1-ounce letter back then. Does anyone have a guess about how much a 1-ounce letter cost to mail back in 1917?"

The students made several guesses: "Six cents." "One cent." "A nickel." "Three cents." "Two cents."

"I have a list of the postal rates charged since 1917," I said. "The post office has been charging for 1-ounce letters since 1885, but this list starts with 1917." I placed a transparency of the list on the overhead projector for the class to see. (See the blackline master on page 152.)

Postal Rate History

The chart below shows the cost to mail a 1-ounce First Class letter in the United States since 1917. Based on the information in the chart, predict the cost of mailing a 1-ounce First Class letter in 2001. Explain your reasoning.

November 3, 1917	3 cents
July 1, 1919	2 cents
July 6, 1932	3 cents
August 1, 1958	4 cents
January 7, 1963	5 cents
January 7, 1968	6 cents
May 16, 1971	8 cents
March 2, 1974	10 cents
December 31, 1975	13 cents
May 29, 1978	15 cents
March 22, 1981	18 cents
November 1, 1981	20 cents
February 17, 1985	22 cents
April 3, 1988	25 cents
February 3, 1991	29 cents
January 1, 1995	32 cents

"As you can see, the price of a 1-ounce letter in 1917 was 3 cents," I said. "How long ago was that? Try using mental math to figure out how many years have passed from 1917 to 1995."

After a minute or so, many hands were wiggling in the air. I called on Ursula.

"I think it was 78 years ago," she said. "I started with 1995 and went back decades. Like 1995, 1985, '75, '65, '55, '45, '35, '25, '15, and that makes 80 years. But I have to subtract 2 years because I went back to 1915, so I got 78 years ago."

"Did someone solve it a different way?" I asked.

"I added 3 to 17 to make 20," explained Jeremiah. "Then I added on 10s from 20 to 90 which made 70. Then I added 5 years to get to 1995 and, with the 3 I added before, it makes 78 years ago."

"I just saw 1995 minus 1917 in my head," said Jackson. "I borrowed and carried and got 78 years as an answer."

No other students had methods to report, so I turned their attention to the list. "Look at the data on the list," I told them. "Talk to someone next to you about these postal rates and see what you notice."

After a few minutes, I asked the students for their attention. I then said, "Raise your hand if you have an observation or question about the list of postal rates."

"From 1917 to 1919 the price went down from 3 cents to 2 cents," said Everett. "Then it went up to 3 cents again in 1932 and then it always went up in price 'til 1995."

"Why are stamps more expensive now?" Moss asked.

"Does anyone have an idea about that?" I asked.

"Taxes have increased and the post office needs more money to operate," Ursula said.

"The workers need more money," added Keith.

"Profit is a reason," said Annie. "Plus, there's more people now than back then."

"I think it has to do with inflation," said Reed.

"Can you explain what you mean by inflation, Reed?" I asked.

"It's when prices are raised," he said.

"It's like when you inflate a balloon," explained Lexie. "The balloon gets bigger. With inflation, things cost more. Prices inflate."

"I have the definition!" exclaimed Reed, waving his dictionary. He read, "Swelling, excess amount of money in circulation."

"I think the cent was worth more in 1917 than it is today," said Cybil. "It's like in Mexico right now. The peso is worth less than it was last year."

"People didn't make as much money then as they do now," added Annie.

"Why did the price of a letter go down from 1917 to 1919?" asked Moss.

"I think World War I was happening then," said Rachel.

"Why would that have an effect on the price of mailing a letter?" I asked.

"Maybe more people sent letters to soldiers in Europe and the post office made so much money that they lowered the price," said Jackson.

"Maybe the price of sending a letter went down in 1919 because of the depression," said Kelsey.

"That's an interesting idea," I replied. "But the Great Depression occurred about 10 years later." I was impressed at the students' knowledge of historical events and how they were linking mathematics with economics and history.

When the students had finished sharing their ideas, I posed a problem for them to solve. Pointing to the list of postal rates on the overhead transparency, I said, "Use the information on this list to predict what the cost might be to mail a 1-ounce letter in the year 2005. Use numbers and words in your explanation, and make a graph that will help explain your reasoning."

"Can we work with partners?" Abel asked.

"You can work with a partner or with your table group," I replied. "But I want each of you to do your own recording."

I passed out a copy of the list of postal rates to each table as well as plenty of 8½-by-11-inch paper. There was a lot of discussion as the students examined the list. Some students looked for patterns, while others began by graphing the information.

As I walked from table to table, I noticed that all the students drawing graphs were making the same error. Most knew to list the dates along one axis of the graph and the prices along the other axis. However, they were listing the dates as they appeared on their postal rate history list—1917, 1919, 1932, 1958, and so on—and not taking into account that the intervals weren't the same. I asked for everyone's attention.

"If you're making a graph, you need to be aware of something very important," I said. "You need to list your dates with equal numbers of years between them. For example, if you choose to list your dates with 10 years in between, they might go like this: 1915, 1925, 1935, 1945, and so on." I wrote these dates on the board.

"If you choose to list every 5 years, they might go like this: 1915, 1920, 1925, 1930, 1935, 1940, and so on." Again, I wrote these dates on the board to help those students who needed to see an example.

"This is important because then you'll have better information about how the jumps in cost related to the years," I added. "Also, when you list the price amounts for the letters on your graph, you need to record those in equal intervals."

When the students returned to work, some revised their graphs while others continued to look for patterns to help them make predictions.

Kelsey called me over to her table and told me that she was excited because she had found a pattern. She read from her paper: *"Yes, I can use this information to predict the cost of a one once first class letter in the year 2005. First, I started to look for a pattern. Then I found a pattern through the hole thing is between 1971-1981. It increced 10 cents. and the same with 1985-1995. So now I predict that it will jumped ten cents more. So it would go to 42 cents."*

Ursula made a chart to organize her data and described her reasoning to me. "In 1965 the price of sending a 1-ounce letter was 5 cents, and in 1975 the price was 13 cents," she said. "This was an increase of 8 cents. Then in 1985, the price was 22 cents. That's an increase from 1975 of 9 cents. Then in 1995, the price is 32 cents, an increase from 1985 of 10 cents. So I predict that the price of a stamp in the year 2005 will be 43 cents, an increase from 1995 of 11 cents. It goes up by 1 cent in what it adds: plus 8, plus 9, plus 10, then I think it will be plus 11 cents."

Reed read from his paper: *"I discarded 1917 to 1971 because they incread steadly by 1 cent. Then for the graph I use the pattern of 1971 to 1981 to find the answer of 44 cents."*

"Can you explain what the pattern was that you used between 1971 and 1981?" I asked.

"Between 1971 and 1974, the price went up by plus 2 cents," he began, "and between 1974 and 1975, the price went up by plus 3 cents. Then between 1975 and 1978, it went up by plus 2; then between 1978 and 1981, it went up by plus 3. Then again in 1981 it went up by plus 2 cents. The pattern for that decade was plus 2, plus 3, plus 2, plus 3, plus 2. So I thought that pattern would repeat itself between 1995 and 2005. That's how I got the answer 44 cents."

Rachel looked at the more recent data starting from 1968 and used estimation to make a prediction. She wrote: *I think, by the year 2005 the price will go up 10¢. The price has escalated around 2¢ every few or couple of years, so by the year 2005 the price for a stamp will be about 41¢.*

The students worked for more than an hour on this problem. When they were finished, several students shared their graphs with the class and

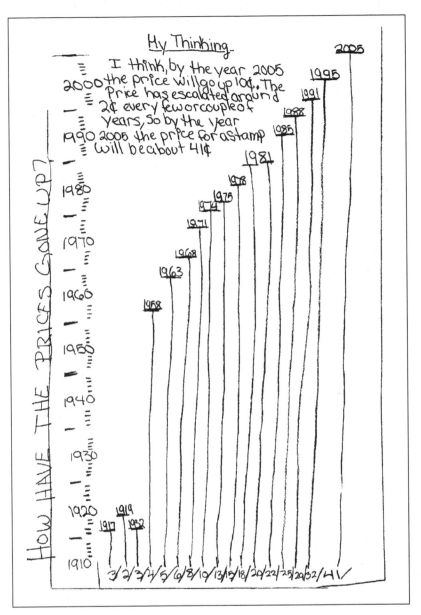

Rachel predicted that a stamp would cost 41 cents because the cost had increased by about 2 cents every few years.

explained how they had arrived at their predictions. When this part of the discussion was over, I asked another question.

"How much has the price of a 1-ounce letter increased since 1917?" I asked. "Figure this out in your heads."

I gave the students a few minutes to think about the problem. Then I said, "Raise your hand if you would like to explain how you solved the problem." Many hands shot up in the air. I called on Esme.

"A 1-ounce letter went up by 29 cents," she said. "The price in 1917 was 3 cents and today's price is 32 cents. I just subtracted 3 from 32 and got 29 as my answer. The price has increased by about 10 times. I know that because 3 times 10 is 30 and that's pretty close to 32 cents."

"Now the postage price is 32 cents, so it's gone up 29 cents," said Ursula. "That's 10½ times what it was in 1912. I know that because 11 times 3 is 33 and 10 times 3 is 30, so it's logical that it would be 10½ times more."

"If you bought a stamp each year it changed price, it would cost you $2.16!" exclaimed Emanuel. "I was just fooling around with the numbers after I finished, and I came up with that."

"Does anyone have any questions or other things to add?" I asked. "What does this problem make you wonder about?"

"What's the answer?" Caitlin asked. "How much will it cost in the year 2005?"

"Nobody really knows what the answer will be," I replied. "That's true of many real-life math problems. Our best answers are just predictions based on the data that we have."

"Yeah, nobody can tell what's going to happen in the future," said Alice.

"We don't know for sure what the price will be," I said, "but we can make a reasonable prediction based on the data that we've analyzed today. For example, would $5.00 be a reasonable prediction for the price of a 1-ounce letter in the year 2005?"

"No!" students chorused.

"How about 50 cents?" I asked.

"Reasonable," the class responded.

"How about 43 cents?" I continued.

"Reasonable," the students repeated.

"We're going to be really old when we finally get to find out how much that letter is going to cost us," said Abel.

"No, we're not!" several students exclaimed.

"Yes, we are!" others responded.

"How old will you be in the year 2005?" I asked.

"It sounds like another mental math problem," giggled Jackson. Everyone laughed. After a minute or so, many hands were waving in the air. I called on Kelsey.

"I'm 10, and 10 plus 10 is 20, so I'll be 20 years old," she said.

"I'm 12 years old now, and it'll be 10 years till 2005, so 12 plus 10 makes 22 years," said Jerome.

"I'm 11, so 11 plus 10 is 21," said Abel. "I guess I won't be too old."

"It will be five years after I'll be able to drive," said Reed.

"You'll be 21 years old!" exclaimed Rachel, laughing.

"In the year 2005, it will be 22 years after I was born!" Ursula announced.

This was a rich mathematical activity because it helped students connect mathematics to the world around them and involved them in looking for patterns in order to make predictions based on mathematical reasoning.

Note: This activity was adapted from one by the Connecticut State Department of Education, 1991.

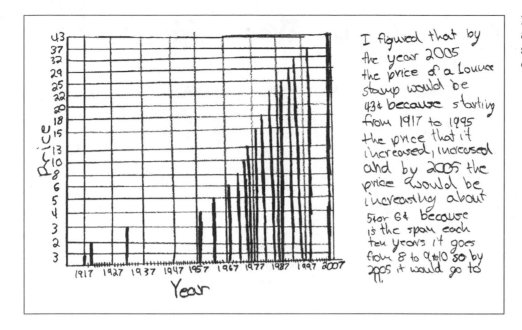

I figured that by the year 2005 the price of a 1 ounce stamp would be 43¢ because starting from 1917 to 1995 the price that it increased, increased and by 2005 the price would be increasing about 5 or 6¢ because is the span each ten years it goes from 8 to 9 to 10 so by 2005 it would go to 11.

Everett drew a graph and predicted that a stamp would cost 43 cents in 2007.

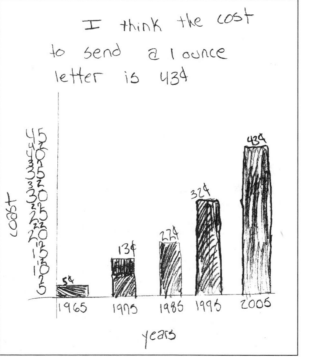

I think the cost to send a 1 ounce letter is 43¢

Alice's graph showed the cost of a stamp every 10 years starting in 1965.

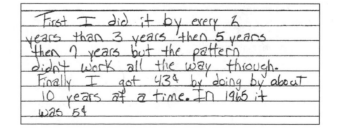

First I did it by every 2 years than 3 years then 5 years then 7 years but the pattern didn't work all the way through. Finally I got 43¢ by doing by about 10 years at a time. In 1965 it was 5¢

On the Day You Were Born

On the Day You Were Born, by Debra Frasier, celebrates life by listing forces in the natural world, "each ready to greet you the very first moment of the very first day you arrived." Colorful wood-block prints accompany a gentle text that describes migrating animals, the spinning earth, the pulling gravity, the flaming sun, the rising tide, and more— each of which was doing something "on the day you were born." At the end of the book, a paragraph describes each natural wonder in simple scientific terms. The lesson based on this book has students explore the number of days that have passed since they were born.

1½ x 2" sticky notes 1 per student

"Do you think we have any birthday twins in our class?" Maryann Wickett asked her fourth grade class.

"What's a birthday twin?" asked Jodie.

"Birthday twins are two people who share a birthday," responded Maryann.

"Do they have to be the same age?" asked Heather.

"No," replied Maryann. "You could be my birthday twin if we both have the same birthday. Raise your hand if you think there are any birthday twins in our class." Most of the students raised their hands.

"How could we find out if we have any birthday twins?" asked Maryann.

"Everyone would have to tell when their birthday is," said Evan.

"Listen as I explain how we'll collect your birthday information," Maryann responded. "Each of you should write your birth date and your name on one of these Post-its." Maryann held up a pad of 1½-by-2-inch Post-its.

"Do we write down the month we were born in and the number of the day?" Jolene asked.

"That's right," Maryann replied. "For example, I'll write my name and May 2. Then I'll stick my Post-it on the board." The students quickly posted the information. Soon the board was filled with 30 yellow Post-it Notes.

"Raise your hand if you have an idea about how to organize our birthday information on the board," Maryann asked.

"Put them in order," suggested Chelsea.

"Explain more about what you mean," said Maryann.

"Put the Januarys together, then the Februarys, and all the way up to December, so we can see if there are any birthday twins," said Chelsea. Maryann hesitated, and Chelsea gave further instructions.

"Just write the months down the side of the board," she explained. "Then you put the Januarys in one row, and the Februarys in another, like that."

Maryann quickly rearranged the Post-its following Chelsea's directions.

"What do you notice about our birthday graph?" Maryann asked.

"Tirina and I are birthday twins!" exclaimed Sandra. Tirina and Sandra were excited to discover that they shared the same birthday. Some students seemed a little disappointed that there was only one pair of birthday twins in the class.

"What else do you notice?" Maryann continued.

"January is the mode. It has the most birthdays," said Yvonne.

"March and June only have one," said Toby. "They have the least."

"December, October, July, April, and February have two," Maya said.

"There are 30 birthdays in all," Alex said.

"January has three more than May, August, September, and November," Alan said.

"January has five more birthdays than March or June," added Jodie.

"February could fit in January three times," Jorge said.

"What questions could we raise after examining the information on the birthday graph? What might you wonder about?" Maryann asked.

"I wonder how it would change if the absent people put their birthdays on the graph," Justine said.

"If Mrs. Martin's class made a birthday graph, would it look the same as ours?" asked Freddie.

There were no more volunteers, but Maryann waited a moment and posed the question again. "What else might we ask or investigate?"

"If we did a graph of the whole school's birthdays, I wonder what the most popular month would be," Oliver said.

"Does the graph tell us who the oldest person in the class is?" asked Kyle.

"No!" others responded.

Maryann then showed the children *On the Day You Were Born* by Debra Frasier and explained that she was going to read it aloud. "I'm going to ask you to solve a mathematical problem when I've finished reading the book," she told the class.

The references to the natural world prompted some students to ask questions. For example, when Maryann read, "On the day you were born gravity's strong pull held you to the Earth with a promise that you would never float away . . . ," Alan raised his hand.

"What's gravity?" he asked.

"Can someone explain what gravity is?" Maryann inquired.

"It's like a magnet," explained Jodie. "The earth is like a magnet that pulls us to it."

After Maryann read, "On the day you were born the Moon pulled on the ocean below, and, wave by wave, a rising tide washed the beaches clean for your footprints . . . ," Maya had a question.

"I don't get it. How does the moon pull?" she asked.

Jolene raised her hand to answer. "That's how we get high tides and low tides," she said.

"There are explanations about your questions at the end of the book," Maryann said. "We can read them after I've finished the story."

After finishing the book, Maryann showed the children the section in the back titled "More about the World around You." She read two parts of the section—"Pulling Gravity" and "Rising Tide"—and told the children they could read other parts on their own if they were interested.

Maryann then raised a question. "How long does it take the Earth to make one complete turn?" she asked. Many hands went up.

"It takes 24 hours for the Earth to turn around. That's a day," said Oliver. Others nodded their agreement.

"How many days do you think have passed since you were born?" Maryann asked the class. The students were quiet, and Maryann asked another question.

"What would you need to know to figure out how many days old you are?"

"I know! I know!" exclaimed Chelsea. "We need to know how many years old we are, then how many days in a year."

"Well, you each know how many years old you are," said Maryann. "Chelsea said you would also need to know how many days there are in a year. How many days are there?"

The responses that Maryann heard startled her. Students suggested 150, 362, 336, 225, 364, and 365. After listening to many guesses, she wrote $365\frac{1}{4}$ on the board.

"How can you have a quarter of a day?" asked Joseph.

"That's why we have leap years," explained Stacy. "When there have been enough quarters, then they add another day."

"The number of quarters they have to have for an extra day is four," said Alan.

"Every 4 years we add an extra day," Maya clarified.

Maryann then listed the months and, with the help of the students, recorded the number of days in each. Again, she was surprised that some children had no idea.

"Can someone describe how you remember the number of days in each month?" Maryann asked.

"I know the '30 days has September' poem," Heather said. "My grandma taught me."

"Say it for us," Maryann urged. Heather did so, and a few children chanted quietly along with her.

"Would someone be willing to write down that poem for others who haven't learned it?" Maryann asked. Alan volunteered.

"I know another way," Oliver said. He made a fist and explained. "You count knuckles and spaces. You say January and point to a knuckle, then February to a space, then March on a knuckle." Oliver demonstrated for the class. July landed on the last knuckle, and he explained how you start over again. "August goes on the same knuckle as January. The knuckles all have 31 days, and the others have 30, but you just have to remember about February."

Maryann then gave directions. "Use this information to figure out how many days old you are," she said. "You may work by yourself or with a partner." The students began to work.

"You get a calculator and I'll get the paper," Alex said to Elvis as the two boys excitedly got started.

"Let's figure out your age and then my age," Kyle suggested to Toby.

"Do you think Mrs. Wickett could be a million days old?" Jamie whispered to Chelsea.

Heather overheard and chimed in, "I doubt it!"

Rick and Alan were exchanging ideas. "You have to multiply by 365," suggested Rick, reaching for a calculator.

"But that's not exactly all," said Alan. "My birthday is June 8, so I think I have to add more days." This was September 21.

"Oh, man, me, too!" moaned Rick. "How are we going to figure that out?"

"Hm, well, let's look at the months and days on the board. We could add 31 for July, 31 for August . . . but I'm not sure what we do with September," replied Alan.

A moment later Alan exclaimed, "Wait, I know! We add 21 for the 21 days in September and 22 for June."

"Add it all up?" questioned Rick. "How come only 22 in June? It says there are 30 days."

"Well, I subtracted 8 from 30 because my birthday is June 8," said Alan.

Rick didn't seem completely sure about Alan's reasoning, but he watched Alan do his calculation. Then Alan offered to help Rick figure out his, and Rick seemed to appreciate the help.

When all the students were finished, Maryann gathered them on the rug to share their results. Alex and Elvis were excited and wanted to share first.

"I am 3,569 days old," Alex began. "Elvis is 3,328. I'm older."

"Yeah, by 241 days," Elvis said.

"I used the calculator and did math addition," Alex added.

Jodie reported next and gave a detailed explanation. "I added 365 nine times because there are 365 days in a year and I'm 9 years old and that came to 3,285," she reported. "Then I added 21 days in April because my birthday is April 21. Then I added all the days in May, June, July, and August. I added 21 days for September, because today is September 21. That came to 165 extra days. Then I added 3,285 plus 165, and I'm 3,450 days old."

(Jodie's confidence made her reasoning persuasive, and it wasn't until later that Maryann realized that Jodie shouldn't have added 21 days for April, but instead the 9 days that were left in the month from April 21 until April 30. "Sometimes it's hard to play close attention to all the details when I'm concentrating on keeping the class organized," Maryann said. "I talked with Jodie later, and she realized her error.")

Manuel also gave a detailed explanation, carefully explaining all that he did. "I'm 9 years old," he said, "so I did 365 times 9 and got 3,285, and that told me how many days old I was on my birthday. But that was on August 12, so I counted and there were 19 more days in August. And then I added on 20 more days in September to get 39. But Oliver showed me that I had the date wrong and it's September 21, so I added on 1 more and changed the 39 to 40. So I'm 3,325 days old."

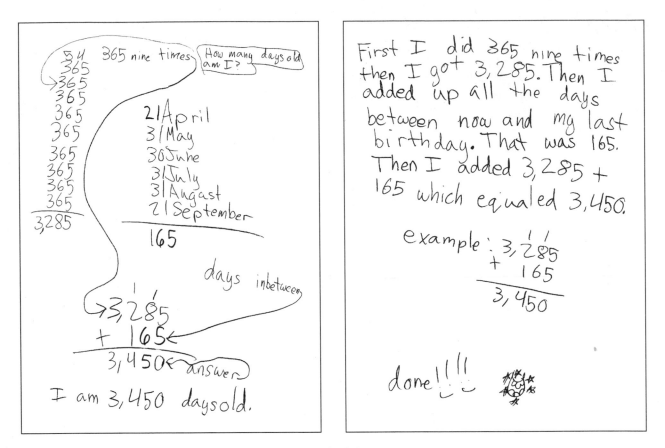

Jodie showed with words and numbers how she reached the answer.

"That was good!" Toby said, impressed with Manuel's presentation.

Stacy volunteered next. "I started like Manuel did," she said. "I multiplied 9 times 365 and that's 3,285. And then I added on 318 more because it's been 318 days since my birthday."

"How did you figure that out?" Maryann asked.

"I counted 47 more days until my next birthday, and I figured out that 318 plus 47 makes 365, which is the whole year. So I added 318 to the 3,285 and got 3,603."

"Mine was a lot easier to figure," Kyle said. "My birthday is on September 12. That was only 9 days ago. So I did 365 times 9 and took away 9. I'm 3,276 days old."

Maryann noticed that none of the students incorporated into their calculations what they had briefly discussed about leap years. "The idea of leap year was new to many of the students, and they seemed to have a good deal to think about for the problem without this information. I decided not to push them to include it," she commented.

The following day, Maryann explained to the children that she was interested in what they thought about this activity. "Write a letter to me telling three things," she said, as she listed three prompts on the board:

How many ~~old~~ days are you?

365 ← days in a year

× 9 ← How old I am

3,285 ← How many days old I was on my birthday

+ 40 ← How many days since my birthday.

3325 ← the answer

I got my answer by using a calculater. On the calculater I pushed The number of days in a year and aded How old I am and got 3,285 I also added from my birtday to now.

How many days old am I

$9 \times 365 = 3285$
day on my birthday

318 Since my birthday

3603
How many days old today

I got 9 because Thats how old I was turning and 365 from how many days in a year

I got 318 becuse thar is 47 more days untell my birthday and 318 + 47 = 365.

1. What did you like about the birthday investigation?
2. What did you learn?
3. Write about something from this activity that you wonder about.

Kyle wrote: *I learned how to find how many days old I was. It was totally fun. And we learned some math. It was like a present. But it was difficult. I still think it is fun.*

Alan wrote: *I learned about how many days are in a year. I wonder how you have all your information and you can put it all together to get your answer. I wonder how it works.*

Stacy wrote: *I wonder if we added everones number in are class up how much it would be I guss 100,000.*

Joseph wrote: *I like it because it was complcated. I Wonder: If ther is enyone else that has the Same Birthday as me.*

Jodie wrote: *I liked using calculators; it improved my math skills and I learned other peoples birthdays . . . I learned how many days I've been alive. I wonder . . . I wonder how many hours I've been alive. (Don't make us figure it out!! Please!!)*

Reflecting on the experience, Maryann reported, "This lesson was successful on two accounts," she said. "It was an opportunity for children to see the usefulness of multiplication. Also, I've been working hard to build the class into a community of learners who cooperate and support one another, and the activity helped encourage this."

A Remainder of One

In *A Remainder of One*, by Elinor J. Pinczes, a troop of 25 bug soldiers line up to march past their queen. The bugs first line up in two groups, leaving soldier Joe alone at the end of the line. The queen "likes things tidy" and is unhappy with a single bug at the end, so Joe has to stand aside and watch the troop march without him. Over the next few days, the bug soldiers line up with three and then four in each line, again leaving out Joe. Finally, the bugs line up with five in each row, "perfect at last—and that's counting Joe." The story leads to an activity in which students use division to solve a number riddle, write their own riddles, and solve those written by their classmates.

Materials
Optional:
Color tiles
25 per student

I read *A Remainder of One* to my class of fifth and sixth graders. They listened intently and were interested in predicting the rhymes in the book. After reading the first several pages, I deliberately began leaving sentences unfinished so that the students could guess the rhyming word. For example, I read: "All 25 soldiers marched past the bug crowd, nervously hoping they'd make their queen _____."

"Proud!" the students chorused.

When I finished reading the part where the 25 bugs lined up in four rows of 6, again leaving "oddball Joe" as a remainder, I posed a question.

"How could the 25 bugs line up so that poor Joe isn't left as the remaining bug?" I asked. Many hands went up. I called on several students to give their ideas.

"They could line up in five rows of 5," Naomi said. "That's 5 times 5 without a remainder."

"I think they should line up in one big line," added Dean. "That would be 25 times 1 and no remainder."

"If I were those bugs, I wouldn't listen to that old queen!" exclaimed Tamar. Everyone laughed.

When I finished reading the book, I asked the class for comments.

"Lots of words in the story rhyme," said Elias.

"It's kind of like division and multiplication," Quinn said.

"Explain what you mean," I said.

"Well, the bugs are kind of dividing themselves up into rows, and sometimes there's a remainder like in a division problem and sometimes there isn't like at the end of the story," she explained. "And we used multiplication when we were guessing what would happen next, like 5 times 5 equals 25."

I then said, "What I'd like to do now is have someone else read the story aloud so that I can record on the board what happens mathematically, kind of how Quinn explained." Volunteers raised their hands, and I called on Sterling since he was the "person of the day," responsible for helping the teacher. As Sterling read, I recorded division sentences on the board to describe the events in the story. I wrote:

$$25 \div 2 = 12 \, R \, 1$$
$$25 \div 3 = 8 \, R \, 1$$
$$25 \div 4 = 6 \, R \, 1$$
$$25 \div 5 = 5 \, R \, 0$$

"Raise your hand if you can explain the first sentence I wrote," I then said. I waited until almost everyone's hand was raised. Then I called on Katherine.

"Twenty-five is the number of bugs, and they divided themselves into two rows," she explained. "That would make 12 bugs in each row with 1 left over as a remainder."

"Katherine's explanation makes sense to me," I said. "Talk in your groups to make sure you all understand what Katherine said. And then discuss the other sentences I wrote on the board to make sure you understand them, and can tell how they are related to the story." I gave the students a few minutes to talk among themselves. I circulated and listened, satisfying myself that they understood how the division sentences related to the story. Then I called them back to attention.

"I now have a riddle for you to solve that relates to the story and the division statements," I began. "Remember that in the story 25 bugs lined up in different ways. In my riddle, I'm thinking of another number of bugs and I'll give you clues to help you guess it. My number is between 1 and 25." I posted a sheet of chart paper on which I had written seven clues:

1. When you divide my number by 1, the remainder is 0.
2. When you divide my number by 2, the remainder is 0.
3. When you divide my number by 3, the remainder is 1.
4. When you divide my number by 4, the remainder is 2.
5. When you divide my number by 5, the remainder is 0.
6. When you divide my number by 6, the remainder is 4.
7. When you divide my number by 7, the remainder is 3.

After the students read the clues, I asked them to discuss the clues with the people at their table. After about a minute, I called for their attention.

"What do you know so far?" I asked. "I'm not interested in an answer yet, but in the information you've gathered by looking at the clues."

"Well, the first clue really didn't help us because if you divide any number by 1 you get a remainder of zero," said Isaac.

"Are you sure?" I asked.

"I think," Isaac replied.

"Let's try 24," I said. "What's 24 divided by 1?"

"Twenty-four!" the students chorused.

"Remainder?" I asked.

"Zero!" they replied.

"Later you can investigate Isaac's general statement to see if it's always true," I said.

"We know that your number is an even number because there's a remainder of zero when you divide it by 2," said Cecilia. "When you divide an even number by 2, there's no remainder. When you divide an odd number by 2, you'll get a remainder," she said.

"What else do you know?" I probed.

"Your number isn't divisible by 3," said Jacob. "We know that because your clue says that when you divide your secret number by 3, there's a remainder of 1."

"Your number is divisible by 5," said Nima. "There's no remainder when you divide it by 5."

"Work in your groups to solve my remainder riddle," I told them. "When you're satisfied that you have the answer, each of you should write a remainder riddle of your own for any number between 1 and 25. Your riddle should have seven clues, just like mine. Use my clues from the chart as a model. Copy them and just put in the correct numbers for the remainders for your secret number."

"Do we write our secret number on the back of our paper?" asked Shane.

"That's a good idea," I replied. "When you're finished, exchange papers with a friend and see if you can solve each other's riddles."

The students dove into solving my remainder riddle. Most groups wrote the numbers from 1 to 25 on their papers and eliminated numbers as they read my clues. Some also wrote division problems to check their numbers, while others figured mentally. Soon, the classroom was buzzing.

"It's 10!" several students shouted out, unable to contain themselves. As soon as they discovered the answer, students began writing riddles of their own. I circulated to give help as needed.

Sterling was having trouble writing the clues for his riddle. He had chosen the number 20 as his secret number, but had no idea about what to do next.

"What's 20 divided by 1?" I asked him. He said that he didn't know how to divide very well. Mathematics is difficult for Sterling, and he lacks confidence. He wasn't sure he could represent division symbolically, and he was hesitant to try.

"If you had 20 cookies and only one person, how many cookies would that person get?" I asked. He still didn't know. I showed Sterling how to write $20 \div 1$ and asked him to get 20 Color Tiles to work with.

"You can use the tiles to show 20 divided by 1 by putting all 20 tiles in one pile," I instructed. "How many are there in the pile?"

"Twenty," he responded.

"Any remaining?" I asked.

"No," he said.

"So that means that 20 divided by 1 equals 20 with a remainder of zero," I said. I recorded this on Sterling's paper.

"Let's do 20 divided by 2," I then said. "Divide the tiles into two equal piles." Sterling formed two groups quickly, using both hands to move two tiles simultaneously.

"How many in each pile are there?" I asked.

"Ten," Sterling responded. He was sure about this without having to count.

"How many remaining?" I asked.

"None," Sterling answered.

"Can you write the division sentence that describes what we just did?" I asked.

"I'm not sure," Sterling said.

"Do it the way I did for putting the tiles into one pile, but write 20 divided by 2 instead, since they're in two piles," I instructed.

"Like this?" Sterling said tentatively, and he correctly recorded $20 \div 2 = 10$.

"There aren't any remaining," I said, "and?"

"Oh, I know," Sterling interrupted, and added $R = 0$ to the sentence. I was going to tell Sterling that he didn't really have to write the remainder when it's zero, but I decided instead to keep him focused on recording division sentences in a systematic and consistent way. Also, by recording $R = 0$, Sterling would understand how to write the clues for a remainder riddle.

"Let's divide the tiles into three groups," I said. Sterling did this, counted the tiles in each group, and successfully recorded $20 \div 3 = 6\ R2$. I watched him do 20 divided by 4, and then left him to continue. Sterling was able to complete the division sentences and write the clues for his remainder riddle.

While Sterling still needed concrete materials to make sense of division, others found the riddles easy to write and wanted a challenge right away.

"Can our secret number be larger than 25?" Naomi asked.

After using Color Tiles to help make sense of the numbers, Sterling wrote a remainder riddle for the number 20.

when you divide my number by 1, remainder is 0

when you divide my number by 2, remainder is 0

when you divide my number by 3, remainder is 2

when you divide my number by 4, remainder is 0

when you divide my number by 5, remainder is 0

when you divide my number by 6 remainder is 2

when you divide my number by 7 remainder is 6

"Choose a secret number between 1 and 25 first, so that we'll have easier riddles to solve," I said. "Then you can choose a larger number for a second riddle."

When all of the students had finished writing their riddles and some had started second ones, I asked for their attention.

"Raise your hand if you have any suggestions for solving a remainder riddle," I said.

"It helps if you write the numbers from 1 to 25 on your paper so you can cross out ones that don't fit the clue," suggested Brooke.

"I had to try each number one at a time starting from 1," said Cesar. "I read each clue and tried it out on each number. When a number didn't fit the clue, I crossed it out."

"After I read clue number 2, I could eliminate either all the odd numbers or all the even numbers," said Quinn. "That got rid of half the numbers."

"It helped me to write out the division problem on another paper and solve it to see what kind of remainder there would be," said Meryl. "It was neat. I used what we learned in division to solve the riddle."

"Now that you've had some experience solving a remainder riddle and also writing one, I want you to solve a friend's riddle," I instructed.

Remainder Riddle

1. When you divide my number by 1, the remainder is 0.

2. When you divide my number by 2, the remainder is 0.

3. When you divide my number by 3, the remainder is 0.

4. When you divide my number by 4, the remainder is 2.

5. When you divide my number by 5, the remainder is 3.

6. When you divide my number by 6, the remainder is 0.

7. When you divide my number by 7, the remainder is 4.

Meryl wrote a remainder riddle for the number 18.

Students paired up to exchange riddles. All were engaged, jotting down numbers on their papers and reading clues. After they solved each other's riddles, they sought out others to exchange with.

Isaac was one of the students who wanted a challenge and wrote a remainder riddle for a larger number. He chose 63 as his secret number:

1. *When you divide my number by 1, the remainder is 0.*
2. *When you divide my number by 2, the remainder is 1.*
3. *When you divide my number by 3, the remainder is 0.*
4. *When you divide my number by 4, the remainder is 3.*
5. *When you divide my number by 5, the remainder is 1.*
6. *When you divide my number by 6, the remainder is 3.*
7. *When you divide my number by 7, the remainder is 0.*

"Why do we have to write seven clues for our riddles?" Isaac asked me.

"That's a good question," I said. "I want to be sure that there are enough clues so that the riddle has only one possible answer."

"What do you mean?" Isaac said.

I answered, "Well, suppose I just gave three clues: When you divide by 1, the remainder is 0; when you divide by 2, the remainder is 0; when you divide by 3, the remainder is 0."

"That's not hard," Isaac said. "It has to be even, and you have to be able to divide it by 3, so it's 6."

"I agree that 6 fits my clues, but it could also be 12 or 18," I said.

Isaac thought about that for a moment. "Oh, yeah," he said. "So I need another clue."

"For some numbers, three clues might be enough," I added. "But for others, you need more. If you do all seven clues, then I'm sure any riddle for numbers up to 100 will have only one answer."

Shane was trying to solve Isaac's riddle and was having trouble. I gave him a 1-to-100 chart so that he could cross out numbers as he eliminated them. Shane began to notice some patterns that helped him.

"Hey," he exclaimed. "I can eliminate half the numbers when I cross out the even ones!" It took Shane a while, but he finally solved Isaac's riddle.

From my discussion with Isaac and watching Shane struggle, I realized that there was a lot more about the mathematics of divisibility to investigate with these students. However, I wanted the students to have a good deal of experience with these riddles first. Their experience would give them a chance to make discoveries that could help them then construct ideas about divisibility. In the meantime, the activity gave them practice with basic division facts and, for a few students, helped them understand the concept of division.

Sam Johnson and the Blue Ribbon Quilt

In *Sam Johnson and the Blue Ribbon Quilt,* by Lisa Campbell Ernst, the women of Rosedale won't allow Sam to join their quilting club, so he forms the Rosedale Men's Quilting Club. Both clubs sew quilts for the county fair contest, and when both quilts fall in the mud, Sam devises a way to save the day—the two groups sew together the undamaged pieces of both quilts into one large patterned quilt, which wins first prize. After reading the book and looking at the various quilt patterns, students explore ideas in geometry as they work together to make paper quilts and write quilt riddles.

Materials:

6" squares of white construction paper 1 per student

3" squares of dark construction paper 2 per student

3" squares of light construction paper 2 per student

"**I** have a book I want to share with you today," I told my fifth and sixth grade students. "Just by looking at the cover, what do you think the book is about?" The cover showed a bearded man perched on a fence with a dog at his side, looking over a valley.

"A farm," said Stan.

"An old man," added Jeffrey. "Maybe it's about the old man's life."

"It's about a blue ribbon quilt," said Muriel, referring to the title. "Maybe it's about a man who makes a quilt from blue ribbons he gets at the fair."

I started reading the story and stopped after the first few pages, just after Sam's wife arrived home and Sam told her that he'd like to join her quilting club.

"Who knows what a quilting club is?" I asked the class.

"They must make quilts," Jasmine answered.

"Yes," I answered. "People work together to make one quilt. Do you know what a quilt is?"

"It's like a big blanket with different colors, made out of patches," explained Giorgio.

"It has two layers. It's a blanket made out of little pieces of rags," said Ashton.

I continued reading the book until I reached the point when the women in the Rosedale Women's Quilting Club laughed at Sam when he asked to join.

"How do you feel about men sewing?" I asked the class.

"It seems kind of weird," Stan said.

"I don't know," Jasmine responded. "I read a book once that was about a tailor, and I think most tailors are men and they sew."

"I think it's okay for men to sew," Jaime said. "Why not?"

I returned to reading. The students enjoyed the story and especially liked that the men and women competed against one another to make quilts for the contest at the fair. They were impressed with the quilt that the men and women put together at the end to solve their problem.

When I finished reading the book, I asked the class for comments.

"I noticed that around each page there was a neat border," said Xavier.

I turned to the last page in the book and read the information about the border patterns: "The border designs in this book are actual quilt patterns, each relating to the content of its particular picture." I showed the class the opening page of the book and told them that this border was called "Open Book." Then I turned to page 20.

"What do you suppose this border is called?" I asked.

Many hands shot up in the air. "Spools of Thread!" several students called out, referring to the neatly placed spools that bordered the illustration.

"That's right," I said. "What else can you say about the story?"

"Well, usually it's women who are protesting for equal rights, and in this book it's men who are," observed Mimi.

"What do you think the author's message is?" I asked.

"I think the author is trying to tell us that cooperation is a good thing," said Ashton.

"I think the message is that men and women are equal and that people should work together," said Sonja.

I then gave the class directions about what to do. "In the story, the men and women of Rosedale worked together to make quilt patches, and then put the patches together to make a quilt," I said. "I'd like to show you a way to make a paper quilt patch and then put four quilt patches together to make a larger quilt pattern."

I held up the paper squares I had prepared. "Each of you needs a 6-by-6-inch white construction paper square," I said. "You also need some 3-by-3-inch squares—two squares each of two different colors."

I gave further directions. "What you're going to do is fold each colored square on the diagonal and cut it in half to make triangles," I explained as I demonstrated folding and cutting one triangle. "All the triangles will be *congruent*. That means that they'll be the same size and shape and would match exactly if I placed one triangle on top of another." I knew that some of the students needed to have the idea of congruence explained, while to others my explanation was merely a reminder.

"If I cut all four little squares in half, how many triangles will I get?" I asked.

"Eight," several students answered.

"Once you cut your triangles, you need to fit them inside the white square like a puzzle. You can't overlap the triangles," I instructed. "Who would like to try doing this for the class?"

The students watched as Julian demonstrated one way to make a quilt pattern with the eight triangles. He carefully placed the triangles into the white square.

"Raise your hand if you can imagine another way to fit the triangles into the white square," I said. Many hands went up. I didn't have any other students demonstrate. Instead, I gave them directions for continuing with the activity.

"You'll work in groups of two, three, or four," I directed, "and explore making patterns with the triangles. Make several quilt patch designs without gluing them down. When you find a design that all of you like, then each of you should make the same design by gluing down triangles on a 6-by-6-inch white square. Each group should make a total of four patches that look exactly the same." Some of the students reached for squares to get started, but I stopped them to give the rest of the directions.

"When your patches are complete," I said, "then put them together into a larger square design. Each group will make a quilt like this one I made, and then we'll compare the different patterns you made." I held up the sample quilt patch I had made.

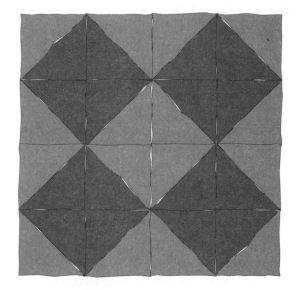

These students had been studying geometry for several weeks. They had explored the ideas of congruency and symmetry and had learned the names and characteristics of different polygons. Two students were new to the class, however, and hadn't had the same experiences as the rest of the students. For them, this activity was an introduction to geometric ideas and vocabulary.

As I observed the students working, I noticed that some students found it easy to flip and rotate their triangles to fit on the white square. Other students, however, found the task difficult and struggled to arrange the triangles so that they covered the white square completely without overlaps.

As the students completed their individual patches, they began to discuss and explore different ways to combine and tape together their patches into one large quilt. After about an hour, all of the quilts were posted on the board in the front of the room.

The Next Day

"Yesterday you made your quilts," I said to the class and pointed to the quilts posted on the board. "Today we're going to look at our quilts as mathematicians." I posted the quilt I had made. (See page 125.)

"Can anyone make an observation about my quilt patch that has to do with geometry?" I asked.

"It has parallel lines," Ashton offered. "There are four sets of parallel lines." Ashton came up and pointed with his finger to show what he noticed.

"There are five shapes that look like jewelry," observed Jasmine. "They're diamonds."

"If you rotated those diamonds, what geometric shape would you have?" I asked.

"Squares!" answered several students.

"I see lots of quadrilaterals," said Jaime.

"What is the definition of a quadrilateral?" I asked.

"It has four sides, four angles, and it's a closed shape," answered Jaime.

"What else do you notice about my quilt?" I probed.

"It has a line of symmetry," answered Stan. "Can I come up?"

"Yes," I responded.

"If you fold it in half this way," he said, showing a line down the center of my quilt, "it's symmetrical, like a butterfly."

"What else?" I asked the class after Stan had sat down.

"One side of the quilt is the same as the other side," observed Mimi. "If you picked up one side and put it on top of the other side, they match perfectly. They're congruent."

As each student made an observation, I recorded the information on the board next to my quilt design. When we were finished, I had written:

Parallel lines
Shapes that look like jewelry
Squares
Quadrilaterals
Symmetrical
Congruent

I then began a discussion about riddles.

"Who can describe what a riddle is?" I asked. Many hands shot up.

"It's like a secret that you give clues to," said Julian. "An animal riddle would be like this: It's a king and it has a mane and only the females hunt for food. Oh, and they're carnivorous!"

"A lion!" several students guessed.

"That's an example of an animal riddle," I said. "You're going to work in your group to write quilt riddles using geometric clues about your quilts. When you're all finished writing your riddles, we'll read them and try and match them with the quilts."

"Before you write your riddles, I'm going to give each group a piece of paper," I said. "I want you to look at your quilt and write down all the things you notice about it. Use as many geometry words as you can to describe your quilt. When you're finished, use your notes to help you write the clues for your quilt riddle. Also, think of a name for your quilt."

the hour Glass
It has 2 lines of symmetry
1 from the middle of the sides to the oposite.

2 It has 2 bowties that are Blue and yellow.

3 It has a Big blue Square in the middle

4 It has 14 large triangles made from the Small blue and yellow triangles.

Muriel, Suzannah, and Lindsey found everyday objects and geometric shapes in their quilt pattern.

As I circulated, I noticed that everyone was busy writing down observations and rotating the designs, trying to identify as many geometric properties in the quilts as possible. The students worked together to find appropriate names for their quilts. For many, finding a name for their patch was a good start for writing their clues.

Jasmine and Sonja were discussing their patch while I was observing.

"These are equilateral triangles," said Sonja.

"No, they're not," argued Jasmine. "Equilateral triangles have sides that are all the same size."

"Well, I know our patch is not symmetrical, because when you fold it in half, the two sides don't match," Sonja said.

I didn't intervene, but listened to their arguments and made mental notes about what they knew about their quilt. Over the year, I add to my information about what students do and don't understand from the many opportunities I have to observe them. From my mental notes, I often jot down information on Post-it Notes and put them in a student's folder. This sort of information helps me when I'm sharing student progress with parents. It also serves as a guide for conversations I need to have with students about certain mathematical ideas.

In their riddles, the children described objects such as faces, houses, school colors, and windmills. At the same time, they included geometric vocabulary such as symmetrical, triangle, trapezoid, congruent, hexagon, and parallelogram.

When the students finished their quilt riddles, they posted them at the front of the room. I asked them not to post their riddles next to their quilts so that we would have the challenge of matching riddles and quilts. I numbered the quilts to make it easier to identify them.

"You're going to take turns reading your riddles to the class," I said. "Please let each group read all of their clues before guessing."

Julian and Judd went first. They read: *"1. It has five shapes of diamonds. 2. There are four blue windmills. 3. There are for purple windmills. 4. There are 6 squares with at least 8 triangles. 5. It has 2 lines of symmetry on the diaganal. It's name is 'Triangle Checkerboard.'"* After several tries, the students guessed the correct quilt.

Jane and Megan went next. They read: *"It has a horizontal line of symmetry. It has a vertical line of symmetry. It has a big blue diamond. It has six triangles. It has four small triangles. It's name is Triangles and Squares."*

The riddle game gave the students the chance to link written descriptions and geometric vocabulary with geometric designs. After a few riddles, the students got better at guessing. Sometimes the name of the quilt gave it away, and sometimes the clues assisted the students.

Marie suggested that we post the quilts in the office with the riddles on a separate piece of chart paper. We did, and the quilt riddles served as a math activity for visitors, students, teachers, and even the school principal!

> La crus
> Hay cihco cuadritos y cuatro Remolinos azules y Hay cuatro Remolinos morados.
> Hay una equix.
> Dos esquinas Tienen el mismo color.

Gareth and Schuyler named their pattern "The Cross" (La Crus). Translation: *There are five little squares and four blue windmills and four purple windmills. There's an X. Two corners have the same color.*

The 329th Friend

> *The 329th Friend*, by Marjorie Weinman Sharmat, tells the story of
> lonely Emery Raccoon who has no friends, so he invites 328 strangers
> to lunch in the hope of making a new friend. Emery peels 329 pota-
> toes, picks 329 bunches of vegetables, and bakes 329 tarts. He set his
> tables with 329 spoons, forks, and knives. The guests arrive "one by
> one and in pairs, threes, fours, fives, tens, twenties, and fifties." As they
> eat, the animals ignore Emery. When he can't find anyone to listen to
> him, he takes his lunch, goes inside his house, and eats by himself. At
> the end of the day, he says good-bye to his guests and cleans up,
> washing "three times 329 which is 987" dishes and glasses and 1,974
> pieces of silverware. He realizes that he found a good friend that
> day—himself. In a lesson based on the book, students make estimates
> and figure out the number of objects Emery worked with.

Pat Feist introduced me to her fourth graders as the guest math teacher. I
recognized a few smiling students who were in my third grade class the
year before. They made me feel at home.

"I want to share a book with you this morning about a raccoon who doesn't
feel very good about himself," I told the class as I held up the cover of *The
329th Friend.*

I continued, "The raccoon doesn't have any friends, and he's very lonely.
He decides to have a party and invite lots of animals to lunch. How many
animals do you suppose he invited to his house?"

"I think he invited 329," Neil said.

"Why do you think that, Neil?" I asked.

"Because the title of the book is *The 329th Friend*," he replied.

LaShon raised her hand. "I think he's going to invite 328 animals because
he's the 329th friend," she said.

"I'm going to begin reading *The 329th Friend* to you. At a certain point,
I'm going to stop reading and ask you a mathematical question," I told the
class.

The children listened carefully as I read each page leading up to Emery
Raccoon's party. They laughed as I read that Emery peels 329 potatoes,
cooks 329 eggs, and cuts up one dozen bed sheets into neat little squares
for napkins. They felt sad for Emery when he is ignored by the other animals
at lunch. The children were delighted when Emery discovers that he has a
friend who has been with him all along—himself!

I read through the part where Emery says good-bye to all of his guests. I said to the class, "I have a question for you. Would you rather spend your time alone or with friends?"

Most of the children wanted to spend time with friends. Only four chose to spend time alone.

"What did you learn from the story?" I asked the class. "What do you think the author's message was?"

"To share with your friends," said Stefano.

"That you need to do something for someone if you want to have friends, something nice," added Jeanine.

"I learned that you can be your own friend," Holly said.

"When Emery's friends had left the house, he had a big mess to clean," I reminded the class. I picked up the book and read what Emery said to himself: "'Everybody used a main dish and a dessert dish and a glass. That's 3 times 329,' he said." Although Emery goes on to give the answer of 987, I didn't read that part.

"What do the numbers 3 and 329 have to do with the story?" I asked. I waited until several children had raised their hands. I called on Blaine.

"The 3 signifies the dishes and the 329 signifies the guests," he said. This response was typical of Blaine, who uses precise language and a touch of humor whenever possible.

"How many dishes did Emery have to wash?" I then asked. "How could you solve this problem?"

"You could add 329 three times," said Ariel.

"You could do 9 three times, 2 three times, and 3 three times," explained Lynette. Although Lynette's explanation was not mathematically correct, none of the other children commented, and I didn't take the time to correct it. I decided to talk privately later with Lynette.

Jameson chimed in, "Or take 300 three times and 29 three times."

I explained to the class that I wanted them to make an estimate first and then figure out how many dishes Emery had to wash. I told them they should explain their reasoning with words and numbers. "You can also use pictures," I added, "if they help explain your thinking."

The students were already seated in groups of four, so I told them that if they needed help, they could ask someone at their table.

As the children started to work, I walked to each table to check if everyone recorded an estimate first. I was interested in seeing what their sense was for 329×3. Most of the students' estimates were in the 900 range, with two exceptions: Kadijah's estimate was 4,000 and Kasey's was 103.

I asked Kasey if she could explain her estimate to me. She just looked at me and shrugged. "I don't know," she said. I was curious to see how Kasey would figure the answer.

Even though the children had been introduced to multiplication, many were more comfortable with using addition to solve the problem. Most of the students solved the problem by adding 329 three times; a few used multiplication. As I approached Stefano, however, I noticed he was busy covering his paper with circles, putting three little dots in each one. I asked him to explain his method to me.

"I'm drawing 329 circles for the animals and three dots each for the things they got dirty," he said.

"What made you think of that?" I asked him.

"I learned it last year. We played a game called Circles and Stars where we multiplied numbers," he told me. Although this method was time-consuming and inefficient for this situation, it made sense to Stefano because he made a connection between this problem and what he learned last year. I made a mental note that Stefano would benefit from seeing different ways to solve this problem.

Patricia solved the problem by correctly adding 329 three times to get 987. She then explained her solution by writing: *I added 9 + 9 + 9 and I got 27. And I added 2 + 2 + 2 + 2 and I got 8. Then I added 3 + 3 + 3 and I got 9. And then I got 987.* Patricia got the correct answer, but I wasn't certain that she understood that the 2s she was adding were really 20s and that the 3s stood for 100s.

In contrast, Veronica's explanation showed an understanding of place value, but she made an addition error. She wrote: *I added 300 + 300 + 300 that was 900. Thene I added 20 + 20 + 20 that was 60. Thene I added 9 + 9 + 9 that was 27. Thene I added all together and that was 997.*

Patricia's and Veronica's papers reminded me that correct answers can mask misconceptions, while incorrect answers can sometimes hide understanding. That's why I think it's important to ask students to explain their reasoning, not just give answers.

Marcus used the traditional algorithm for multiplying a three-digit number by a one-digit number. However, he wrote: *I added 329 + 329 + 329 dishes and it added up to 987 dishes.* I watched him as he drew three columns, labeled them "hundred," "ten," and "ones," and drew nine big dishes in the hundreds column, eight medium-sized dishes in the tens column, and seven little dishes in the ones column.

"This is what the answer really means," he explained.

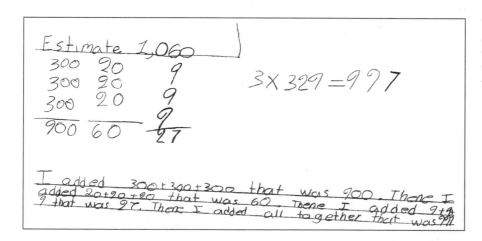

Veronica made an addition error, but her work showed that she understood place value.

As I observed the class at work, I was able to learn about the children's number sense, their understanding of place value, and their facility with addition and multiplication. Some children in the class were able to move directly to a solution; others were totally puzzled.

Neil, for example, was hunched over his paper drawing a row of trees when I came to his table.

"How are you doing with the problem?" I asked.

"I don't understand what to do," he said.

"Did you try to get help from the people at your table?" I asked him.

"No," he said.

I asked him if he knew how many animals there were altogether and how many things each one used. He told me there were 329 animals and they each used three things.

"What do you need to figure out?" I asked.

"How many things he had to wash," Neil answered. "I don't know what to do."

"Neil, I want you to work with Gregario so he can explain his thinking to you. Sometimes what your classmates have to say makes more sense than how an adult says it," I said.

Neil and Gregario teamed up, and I could tell that Gregario relished the idea of being the teacher. In contrast to Neil, Gregario immediately knew what to do when I posed the problem to the class. As I listened, Gregario explained to Neil that each of the 328 guests, plus Emery, used 3 dishes. He helped Neil record and figure the answer to 3 × 329.

Jameson explained his thinking in detail. He wrote: *This is how I got my answer first I added 9 plus 9 plus 9 and it equiled 27 and I put the 7 in the ones and the 20 in the tens and I [got] 87 and then I added 300 plus 300 plus 300 and got 900 and the answer is 987.*

The students finished their work in about 20 minutes. I collected their papers and told them I would return the following day to talk more about Emery and his friends.

Neil explained how to solve the problem using multiplication.

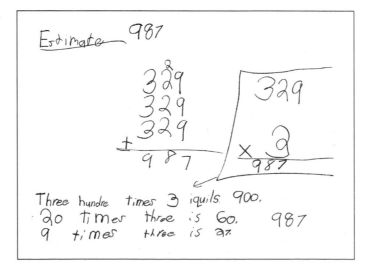

The Next Day

"Yesterday I read you the story of Emery Raccoon," I said, as I began my second lesson with Pat Feist's fourth graders. "You all worked on finding out how many dishes Emery had to wash after his lunch guests left. Would anyone like to share their solutions?"

After the students shared their ideas, I continued reading the story, revealing the correct answer. Some students realized that their solution was incorrect, and several looked disappointed.

"Mistakes happen," I told them, "especially when you're learning. The good thing is that we can learn from our mistakes."

I finished reading the story and then said, "Today I have a new question about Emery and his lunch party." I opened the book to the place where Emery's guests were arriving at his house. I read the part that says that the guests arrived one by one and in pairs, 3s, 4s, 5s, 10s, 20s, and 50s.

Then I asked, "If Emery's guests had come only in pairs, how many pairs would have come to the lunch?" I told the children that they could work alone, with partners, or in groups of four. They got to work.

Jameson made a chart. He wrote: *I got my answer by doing 8 in 2's and I got 4 groups. And then I did 20 in 2's and got 10 groups. After that I did 300 in 2's and [got] 150 my answer is 164.*

Many of the children solved the problem by drawing tally marks and circling pairs, then counting to find out how many pairs they had circled. Irina, for example, explained: *I got the answer by using circles and talley Marks And then just Count the Circles. (each two tally marks stand for pairs of animals)*

Alexis, also drawing circles, said, "I'm going to be here for a million years!"

Lucina solved the problem by counting by 2s, starting with 2, and writing all the numbers up to 328. Then she counted how many numbers she had written, and erroneously reported an answer of 168.

	Estimate 214		total 164
300	20	8	I got my
	2	2	answer by
	4	4	doing 8 in 2's
	6	6	and I got 4
	8	8	groups. And
	10		then I did
			20 in 2's and
			got 10 groups.
			After that
			I did 300 in
total 150	total 10	total 4	2's and 150, my answer is 164.

Jameson used a chart to help find the answer.

Irina used two tally marks inside a circle to represent each pair of animals, then counted the circles.

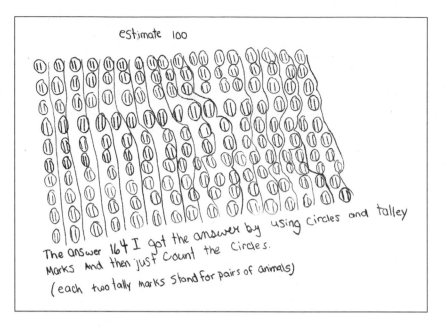

estimate 100

The answer 164 I got the answer by using circles and talley Marks And then just count the circles.
(each two tally marks stand for pairs of animals)

Gregario was able to arrive at the answer within minutes. He first divided 28 in half in his head. He told me, "There's 28, and 14 plus 14 is 28." He then went to the hundreds place. "Half of 300 is 150," he said, "because if there's 30, half of 30 is 15, and I just added a zero when it's 300, and the answer is 150. So I added 14 and 150 and got 164." I asked Gregario to explain his reasoning in writing. He grumbled, but did it. (See below.)

I posed another problem to the few students who finished early. "If Emery's guests had arrived in groups of 50, how many groups would have come to his lunch?" For the few students who tried this problem, figuring out how many 50s were in 328 seemed easier for them than figuring out how many 2s were in 328. They knew that there are two 50s in 100, and they proceeded to 300 with ease, adding the extra 28 as a leftover group.

Gregario preferred to explain his method orally but agreed to write about it.

Theres 28 and
14+14=28 on the
300 its 150 Because
if it's 30, it's 15 and 15,
So I just added a 0 when
it's 300 and 150,
On the 14, I put
the 14, on the 150
and it aquabed 164.

Two Months Later

Too often we jump from one problem to the next instead of allowing children to start from a place where they have some experience. I decided to return to Pat Feist's class two months later and pose the same problem. I was interested in seeing if the students would use the same methods to solve the problem or come up with new strategies.

I began by showing the class the cover of *The 329th Friend*. "Do you remember this book I read to you a few months ago?" I asked. The class responded yes, and I asked Blaine to retell the story.

Blaine retold the story, missing only a few details. Several other students chimed in to add little parts that he left out. The children remembered Emery, and the retelling helped bring us all back to where we left off.

"Do you remember the problem I asked you to solve?" I inquired. Everyone nodded, and I asked Alexis to explain the problem.

"Raise your hand if you remember how you solved it," I told them. About half the students raised their hands.

"Hey!" shouted Gregario. "You gave us copies of the papers, and they're in our desks!" I waited several minutes for the students to retrieve their papers. To my surprise, many of them found their copies.

"Emery had to wash everybody's main dish, dessert dish, and glass," I said. "That was 3 times 329. I forgot to ask you to solve the next problem in the book." I read from the book: "Everybody used a fork, knife, and spoon."

Then I asked, "How many forks, knives, and spoons did Emery have to wash?"

"That's the same problem!" exclaimed Jared.

"I want you to solve this problem using numbers and words. Also, try to solve it using a different method than you used to solve the first problem," I instructed.

The students got right to work. While they were working, I noticed that many of them were approaching the problem the same way they had before, by using repeated addition. When I encouraged them to use another method, almost all of the students multiplied 329×3 successfully. Even though the students could multiply, they still felt more secure with addition and relied on it to solve the problem.

I noted the overall improvement in the class. It was good to see that students who had experienced difficulty the first time around were now able to move directly to a correct solution and explain their thinking.

As the students finished their work, I posed another problem. "How many things did Emery have to wash altogether?" I asked.

Again, most students solved the problem easily, either multiplying 987×2 or adding $987 + 987$. When they were finished, the children shared their work with one another.

One of my goals for students is for them to develop confidence in their ability to do mathematics. Revisiting the Emery Raccoon problem gave these students a chance to build on what they already knew. The students felt more sure of themselves the second time around.

The Twelve Circus Rings

The Twelve Circus Rings, by Seymour Chwast, shows increasing numbers of people and animals performing in circus rings. This book borrows its structure from "The Twelve Days of Christmas," starting with one daredevil in a ring and progressing to a ring full of animals, horseback riders, leapers, jugglers, bears, clowns, and more. After the book is read, the students explore numbers and their relationships as they determine the total number of animals and people both in each ring and in the entire circus.

I held up the cover of *The Twelve Circus Rings*, showing Carole Smith's fourth and fifth graders the picture of a giant elephant surrounded by circus performers.

"Raise your hand if you've been to a circus before," I said. About half the students indicated that they had.

"Raise your hand if you would like to share something you know about the circus," I then said.

"They're made to make you laugh," said Anne-Marie.

"People do crazy things at a circus," said Jansen, "like daredevils do stunts that could kill them."

"There are clowns and lots of animals," Jed added.

"If you've never been to a circus, I have a book that will give you an idea of what a circus is like," I told them. "For those of you who know about circuses, let's see if the circus in my book matches the one you're thinking about. The book is called *The Twelve Circus Rings* and it's written by Seymour Chwast."

I read the book aloud, starting with the first circus ring and progressing through 11 more. The rings become more complex and zany as the numbers of animals and people get bigger and bigger. The students were impressed by the illustrations and made comments throughout the reading.

"Wow, elephants are boxing!" Maggie exclaimed.

"Look at the clowns in tennis shoes!" Federico noticed. Everyone laughed.

"Every time there's a new picture, the elephant is doing something new," Flint commented.

"Ten leapers leaping sounds like 'The 12 Days of Christmas,'" said Arturo.

As I read, I paced my reading to encourage the students to join in the repeating verses—"Five dogs a-barking, four aerialists zooming, three monkeys playing," and so on. When I finished reading the book, I asked the class what they noticed about the mathematics in the story.

"There's a pattern," said Camilla. "The pattern is that the number of animals and people is getting bigger with each ring."

"How many daredevils are there in each circus ring?" I asked.

"One," the class chorused.

"How many daredevils are there in all of the rings put together?" I continued.

"Twelve," the students responded.

"What about the elephants?" I asked. "How many in each ring and how many altogether?" I gave the class a few moments to think. After about a third of the students had raised their hands, I called on Madeleine.

"There are 2 elephants in each circus ring, except for the first ring," she explained. "I think there are 22 elephants altogether."

"How did you figure, Madeleine?" I asked.

"I used multiplication. I did 11 rings multiplied by 2 elephants in each ring," she answered. Other students nodded their agreement.

"I have two mathematical problems for you to solve," I told the class. I wrote the first question on the board and read it aloud:

How many are there of each circus performer?

"Do you mean how many elephants in all of the 12 rings?" Benno asked.

"That's right," I answered. "How many of each circus performer are in the entire circus?"

I then wrote the second question on the board and again read it aloud:

How many circus performers are there altogether?

"So we have to add up every performer in all 12 rings?" Arturo asked.

"Yes, you could add them up," I responded. "How else do you think you might solve the problem?"

"Maybe you could use multiplication like Madeleine did when she figured out the elephants," suggested Camilla.

"You could make a chart with graph paper," said Theo.

"You could draw pictures of all the performers, but that would take a long time," said Federico.

There were no other suggestions, so I continued with directions. "I'll record the names of the performers on the board to help you remember them," I said. I listed the numbers from 1 to 12 on the board and asked the students to recall the performers. I recorded the names of the circus performers:

1 daredevil, 2 elephants, 3 monkeys, 4 aerialists, . . .

I continued until the list was complete, and we checked in the book to be sure we were right.

"You may work together on the circus problem, but I want each of you to have your own recording sheet," I told the students. They got right to work.

Bernardo was using a calculator when I visited his table. He figured the answer to $1 + 2 + 3 + 4 + 5 + 6 + 7 + 8 + 9 + 10 + 11 + 12$ and wrote: *On the sorcis performers thay war 78 animals and porsens.*

Although it was difficult for him, Bernardo chose to write his answer in English. His first language is Spanish, and he had just recently been placed in an all-English-speaking classroom. Bernardo hadn't realized that adding together the circus rings was not a way to the solution. To help refocus him on the problem, I asked him some questions.

"Bernardo, how many daredevils are in the circus?" I asked first.

"There's 1 in each ring, so there are 12," he answered correctly.

"How many elephants do you think there are?" I asked.

"Well, there are 2 in each ring, but they are only in 11 rings," he said.

"So how would you figure out how many in 11 rings?" I asked.

"Use the calculator?" he guessed.

"It's okay to use a calculator, as long as you know what you'd do with it," I told him.

"I could push 2, then plus, then push the equals sign 11 times," he said.

"That's called the 'repeat function,'" I said. "Where did you learn that?"

"At my other school," he said with a smile. Bernardo continued using the calculator to figure how many there were of each performer, and then he added them to arrive at the correct answer of 364 total performers.

Judy made a chart to organize her figures and then used addition to solve the problem. She wrote: *We read a book called 12 Curcus Performers. I made a gragh so I can see what I'm doing. The gragh shows how many performers in each ring. After I made the gragh. The first thing I did was add the same performer in all the rings. After I got the answer to each performer I add all the performers together to know how many performers in the hole performer.*

Judy drew a chart and then explained how she used addition to get the answer.

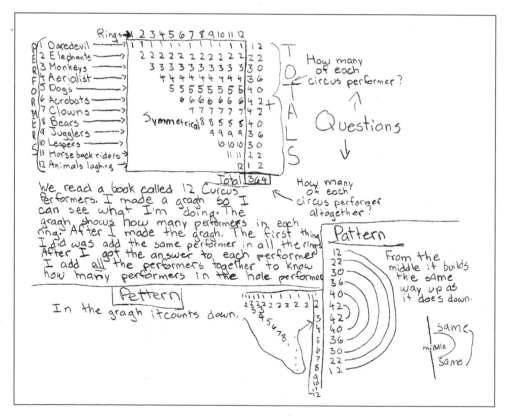

Calie called me over for help. "I'm confused," she said. "I got the answer 42 for the acrobats and also for the clowns."

"How did you get your answers?" I asked.

"I multiplied 6 times 7 because there were six acrobats in seven rings," she answered. "Then I did 7 times 6, for the seven clowns in six rings."

I paused to give Calie a chance to think a bit. "Ooooh," she grinned, "6 times 7 and 7 times 6 are really the same!" She went back to work on her paper.

Flint was using multiplication and addition to solve the problem. He multiplied to find the total number of each performer: 1×12, 2×11, 3×10, and so on. He then wrote: *I used a calculater and added all the numbers and came up with 369.* I looked carefully at his paper, trying to see where he had made an error.

"I don't agree that 6×7 equals 47," I said when I found that calculation.

"Oh yeah," he said when he realized his mistake. He corrected his answer to 364 performers. Flint's work was organized and correct except for the computation error. I knew that his understanding of the problem was solid, but I also wanted him to realize that a correct answer is important.

Flint used a calculator to add up all of the circus performers.

Aubrey and Maggie were sitting next to each other, but they were working separately on the circus problem. I heard them shout, "We found a pattern!" I walked over to their table and asked them what they were excited about.

"We were working, and all of a sudden we both discovered this pattern at the same time!" Maggie exclaimed.

"Tell me about the pattern you discovered," I said.

"We both used multiplication to find out how many of each performer there are in the circus," said Aubrey.

"Explain how you did that," I probed.

"Well, for the daredevils we did 1 times 12 because there's 1 daredevil in 12 circus rings," he explained. "Then we just did the same for the other performers, like 2 elephants times 11 rings, 3 times 10, 4 times 9, 'til we got to the end."

"We found the pattern when we looked at the answers to all the multiplication problems," Maggie added. "Look, the answers to the multiplication problems go: 12, 22, 30, 36, 40, 42, 42, 40, 36, 30, 22, 12. If you look at the numbers in the 1s place, they go: 2, 2, 0, 6, 0, 2, 2, 0, 6, 0, 2, 2. It's a repeating pattern." Maggie went off to share her discovery with Calie.

Maggie was pleased with the patterns she found.

1. How many of each circus performer?

1. Daredevil = 12
2. Elephants = 22
3. Monkeys = 30
4. Aerialists = 36
5. dogs = 40
6. Acrobats = 42
7. clowns = 42
8. Bears = 40
9. Jugglers = 36
10. Leapers = 30
11. Horseback riders = 22
12. Animals laughing = 12

364

2. How many circus performers altogether.
364
I added my ansers from my last ansers.

I multiplied it like on the performer 1 x 12 then 2 x 11 then 3 x 10 then 4 x 9 then 5 x 8 then 6 x 7 then 7 x 6 then 8 x 5 then 9 x 4 then 10 x 3 then 11 x 2 then 12 x 1. The first number represents the performer and the second number represents the circus rings. I also found patterns.

1. 12
2. 22
3. 30
4. 36
5. 40
6. 42
7. 42
8. 40
9. 36
10. 30
11. 22
12. 12

2
2
0
6
0
2
2
0
6
0
2
2

These numbers came from the ansers

After the students had had time to solve the problem, I initiated a class discussion so that students could share their solutions. Several students described the pattern that Maggie and Aubrey had found. In order for the rest of the class to see this pattern, I asked Maggie to read the numbers while I listed them on the board:

12, 22, 30, 36, 40, 42, 42, 40, 36, 22, 12

After Maggie explained where she got these numbers, I asked the students to talk with the others at their tables about the patterns in the list. After a few minutes, several hands were raised. I called on Anne-Marie.

"The numbers go up and then they go down," she said.

"There's a 12 on one side and a 12 on the other," said Bernardo.

"I noticed this pattern when I was doing the problem," Benno said.

"The pattern looks symmetrical," Judy said.

"What do you mean by symmetrical?" I asked.

"It's symmetrical because the numbers on both sides are exactly the same and the number pattern divides in the middle at 42s," Judy explained. She came up to the board and pointed to the space in the middle of the number pattern between the two 42s.

"Now that you've answered the two questions about the circus rings and we've discussed the patterns you found, I'm interested in knowing what else you learned while working on these problems. Talk with the people in your group, and then we'll talk as a class," I said. After a few minutes, I asked for volunteers to report their ideas.

"I learned that some methods are better than others when you're doing a problem," said Jo.

"Explain what you mean," I said.

"I started out making a big chart, but that took too long, so I ended up multiplying, and that was faster and easier," she replied.

"I learned that math answers can turn out to have a pattern that's neat to look at," Ivor said.

"I learned that we could use the answer to the first problem to solve the second problem," added Judy.

"I learned that if you make a graph to organize the numbers, it makes it easier, and you can see a pattern better that way," Theo said.

"I learned that if you're going to use a calculator, you better know what you're doing!" Bernardo exclaimed.

I believe that discussing a lesson is extremely important. Allowing the time for students to reflect on their thinking and learning supports each student's learning. Having students share their ideas with one another helps them think of themselves as mathematicians. Class discussions in which students share their mathematical ideas, opinions, and questions helps to create a classroom culture where children's thinking is valued.

Two Ways to Count to Ten

Two Ways to Count to Ten is a Liberian folktale retold by Ruby Dee. In the story, the leopard, king of the jungle, decides that it's time to find a successor who will eventually become king. He invites animals from far and wide and tells them that he "shall seek the cleverest among you, for your king must be wise." He says that the new prince will be the animal that can throw up a spear and count to 10 before it hits the ground. Animals try and fail. Finally, an antelope throws up the spear and counts to 10 by 2s, winning the contest. After reading this story, students investigate finding the factors of numbers.

Materials: none

One morning, I began class by showing my fifth graders *Two Ways to Count to Ten*. "This is a folktale from Liberia," I said to my fifth graders, "a country in West Africa."

As I read the story, the students waited with anticipation as each animal tried to count to 10 before the spear hit the ground. Some chanted along with me as each animal announced, "I will be king, I can do this thing!"

When I read that the antelope tossed the spear up into the air and called out only five words, some of the students immediately figured out what the antelope said. I heard several whisper, "Two, four, six, eight, ten."

After reading the story, I posed a question for the class. "In the story, the antelope counted to 10 by 2s," I said. "Are there other ways to count to 10?"

Hands shot up, and several students had ideas. "Count by 1s." "Just start with 10 and you're there." "You go 5, 10, and it works." I wrote on the board:

1, 2, 5, 10

"You can count by 3s, too," said Elias. "You go 3, 6, 9, plus 1."

"How is Elias's way different from the other ways you counted to 10?" I asked the class.

"You don't land exactly on 10 using the same steps," said Brittany.

"How about 1, 2, 3, and skip to 10," suggested Abbott.

"That's the same as Elias's," Nima said. "They're not even steps."

I then explained to the class, "When we count to 10 by 1, 2, or 5, we follow a pattern. Once you know the pattern, you're able to predict what the next number will be. If I counted '3, 6, 9,' as Elias did, then it's logical to predict that 12 comes next. I'm interested in investigating ways to count to numbers in predictable patterns."

"So mine isn't right?" Abbott asked.

"The problem with your suggestion is that we could use your method to get to any number," I responded. "It could be 1, 2, 3, skip some, and then 23, or 65, or 7,431." Some of the students giggled; Abbott nodded.

"Today we'll investigate how to count to numbers using what Nima called 'even steps,'" I continued. "For 10, we have four ways of counting, by 1s, 2s, 5s, and 10. How many ways are there for counting to 12?" I wrote the number *12* on the board.

"Talk about this with the person next to you," I directed. After about a minute, at least one student from each group had a hand in the air. I called on Quinn.

"You can count to 12 by 1s, 2s, 3s, 4s, 6s, and 12," she reported. I wrote next to the 12 on the board:

$$1, 2, 3, 4, 6, 12$$

I called on students to demonstrate the numbers to verify that we reached 12 for each with even steps.

"So we have ways to count to 10 and 12," I said. "Now we are going to find all the ways to count to the numbers from 1 to 49."

I pointed to three large charts I had taped to the board. I had ruled each chart into three columns and labeled the columns: "Number," "Ways to Count," and "Number of Ways." On the first chart I had listed the numbers from 1 to 17 in the first column. On the other charts, I had listed 18 to 34 and 35 to 49. (I listed only the numbers to 49 because later in the lesson, I would ask students to find the factors for 50.) I ruled lines across the charts under each number.

I went to the number 10 on the first chart and in the "Ways to Count" column, I wrote *1, 2, 5, 10*. In the "Number of Ways" column, I wrote *4*. Then, next to the number 12, I wrote *1, 2, 3, 4, 6, 12* in the "Ways to Count" column and *6* in the "Number of Ways" column.

Number	Ways to Count	Number of Ways	Number	Ways to Count	Number of Ways	Number	Ways to Count	Number of Ways
1			18			35		
2			19			36		
3			20			37		
4			21			38		
5			22			39		
6			23			40		
7			24			41		
8			25			42		
9			26			43		
10	1,2,5,10	4	27			44		
11			28			45		
12	1,2,3,4,6,12	6	29			46		
13			30			47		
14			31			48		
15			32			49		
16			33					
17			34					

"Who can explain what I recorded?" I asked. I waited until about half of the students had raised their hands and then called on Donna.

"You wrote the starting numbers for counting in the second column, and then counted up how many there are," Donna explained succinctly.

"That's right," I said. Then I explained how they were to investigate numbers.

"You'll work in pairs," I said, "and each pair will investigate as many numbers as you have time to do. You and your partner should find all the ways to count to whatever numbers you choose and record your findings on a sheet of paper."

"When we find all the ways to count to a number, do we record the ways on the chart?" asked Naomi.

"No," I replied, "record just on a sheet of paper. After everyone has figured the ways to count to these numbers, I'll fill in this chart with your ideas."

"Do we have to do the numbers in order?" Eartha asked.

"No," I answered. "Choose ones you're curious about or interested in. Do a variety of some large and some small."

There were no more questions, so I had the students pair up. As I observed the students work, I noticed that they were using different strategies for finding ways to count to their numbers. Some used calculators, some were skip counting, some were multiplying, and others were using division.

A few students were using a strategy based on part of the multiplication unit we had started a few weeks earlier. In one of the multiplication activities, the students had used ½-inch squared paper to create rectangular arrays for the numbers from 1 to 36. For example, for the number 12, they had cut out three rectangles—a 3-by-4, a 2-by-6, and a 1-by-12. I had introduced the word *factor* to describe the numbers used in multiplication to arrive at an answer, or product, and connected the idea of factors to the dimensions of the rectangular arrays.

After about 15 minutes, I asked for the students' attention. "I know you can still do more," I said, "but I'm interested in taking a moment to hear about the different strategies you're using to find the ways to count to a number."

"We were looking at the chart we made for the rectangles," said Brittany.

"How did the array chart help you?" I asked.

"Well, the arrays for 24 are 1 by 24, 2 by 12, 3 by 8, and 4 by 6," Brittany replied. "So I knew you could count by 1, 24, 2, 12, 3, 8, 4, and 6."

"Ooooh, that's neat," Jacob said.

"What's neat?" I asked him.

"How she used the rectangle chart to figure," he responded, and looked to locate one of the numbers he had been working on.

"Yes, the chart of arrays shows that 1, 2, 3, 4, 6, 8, and 12 are all factors of 24," I said to reinforce the use of the word *factor* and connect it to this activity. I used this term as often as possible during the activity to help the children become familiar with it in the contexts of what they were doing and thinking about.

Isaac reported next. "Like for 20, I started with 1 and I know that 1 times any number equals that number, so 1 times 20 equals 20," he said. "Then I went in order. Like 2 times what makes 20? Then 3, then 4, and I kept going like that."

Eartha had a different method. "I used a multiplication chart to see how to count up to a number," she explained.

"I used a calculator," said Jacob. "I did 36, and first I tried 2. I pushed 2, then plus, then I kept pushing the equals sign to see if I would land on 36. I tried that for each number."

"I used division to help me find all the ways," said Nima.

"Can you explain how you used division?" I asked.

"I took 9," she said. "I thought about what you could divide 9 by and not have a remainder. I did 9 divided by 1 equals 9 and 9 divided by 3 equals 3."

"Did anyone use a different method?" I asked.

"With 44, you can keep adding on to find the ways," said Brooke. "I did 4 plus 4 equals 8, 8 plus 4 equals 12, then 12 plus 4 equals 16. I kept adding on to see if I could get to 44 counting by 4s. It worked."

"Any other ways?" I asked the class.

"Well, 46 divided by 2 is 23, so I know I could count by 2s to 46," said Jacob. "And since 23 is half of 46, I can count by 23. You go 23, 46."

"We were investigating the number 38," said Bethia. "Half of 30 is 15, half of 8 is 4, and 15 plus 4 is 19. So you can divide 38 by 19. So I know I can count by 19 and I can count by 1."

"And I know that I can count by 2s because 38 is an even number," her partner, Elias, said.

"From listening to your ideas, I see you have many different strategies for finding the ways to count to a number," I said. "Go back to work, and also think about how you can make sure you have found all the factors or ways to count to your number." The students worked for the rest of math class. I collected their papers and told them that we would continue our investigation the next day.

The Second Day

"I looked over your papers," I said to begin class. "Now I'm going to give them back to you so you can report what you've discovered."

After handing back their papers, I asked who worked on the number 1. Several pairs reported that 1 has only one factor—itself. I walked over to the "Ways to Count" chart, and wrote a *1* under "Ways to Count" and *1* under "Number of Ways."

I continued to call out each number up to 49, recording on the charts the factors for each number and the number of ways to get that number. Filling in the charts in front of everyone was helpful. If several pairs did the same number, they checked to be sure they agreed. When we got to a number that no one had chosen, we investigated it together as a class.

When I had filled in the charts up to the number 36, I stopped to ask a question. "Let's look at the charts so far," I said. "What do you notice? Discuss this with your group, and jot down some of your ideas." After a few minutes, I asked for the students' attention and repeated my question.

"There are prime numbers up there," said Isaac. I had introduced the idea of prime numbers when the students had cut out the rectangular arrays. The prime numbers each had only one rectangle—1 by 13, 1 by 23, and so on.

"Tell us what a prime number is," I said.

"It's a number that has only 1 and itself as factors," he responded. I wrote Isaac's statement about prime numbers on the board.

"Help me list all the prime numbers from 1 to 49," I said to the class. I knew that for some students this would be easy, while others would have difficulty. Having the students respond in unison allowed those who were unsure to listen to the others. I recorded on the board:

2, 3, 5, 7, 11, 13, 17, 19, 23, 29, 31, 37

Then the going got hard because our chart of rectangular arrays went only to 36. Finally, I added *41, 43,* and *47* to the list.

"What do you notice about the possible ways to count for prime numbers?" I asked.

"There are only two ways to count to prime numbers," said Bethia. I recorded her idea.

"That's because prime numbers have only two factors," I said. "What else do you notice about the chart?"

"All the prime numbers are odd except for 2," said Cesar.

"Every number has 1 and itself as factors," said Nima.

"Every even number has 2 as a factor," said Nathan.

I recorded their ideas as they presented them. Then I asked, "What do you notice about the square numbers? What numbers are square numbers?"

"If you look at the rectangular arrays, the square numbers are the ones with cut-out squares," said Brittany. "Like a 3-by-3 square and a 4-by-4 square."

As students called out the square numbers—1, 4, 9, 16, 25, 36—I drew squares around each of them on the charts and then listed them on the board.

"What would the next square number be?" I asked. "Talk to your partner about this."

In a moment, more than half of the students had raised their hands. "Let's say together what the next square is," I said.

"Forty-nine," the students said in unison. I added *49* to the list on the board.

"It's 7 times 7," Eartha added. "We did that number."

"What do you notice about the square numbers?" I asked.

"Square numbers have an odd number of factors," said Isaac. The others checked and seemed surprised by this and impressed that Isaac had noticed it. I recorded Isaac's idea.

"What else do you notice about the chart?" I probed.

"I notice something!" exclaimed Quinn. "If a number ends in zero or 5, one of its factors is 5." I recorded her statement and instructed the students to check the chart to see if that was true. They agreed it was.

"I have one!" Jacob exclaimed. "Every odd number has only odd factors."

I recorded Jacob's idea and then had the class check to see if Jacob's conjecture was true. I pointed to each odd number to be sure that all of their factors were odd numbers. Jacob smiled when we confirmed that he was correct.

"All even numbers have some factors the same as the number that is half of that number," said Elias. "Like 24. Half is 12. The factors for 12 are 1, 2, 3, 4, 6, and 24 has those same factors."

"Elias's observation shows us how some numbers are connected," I said, recording his idea.

No other students had ideas to share, so I continued filling in the chart up to 49. Then I introduced another problem for them to solve.

"I think that your ideas are useful to help you figure out how to find the ways to count to a number," I said. "Try the number 50. Find the factors of 50 and explain how you know each number is a factor. Also, try and explain how you know you have found all the factors."

The students worked for about 20 minutes finding the factors for 50. When most were finished, I asked for volunteers to share.

Nathan wrote: *1 is a factor becaues 1 × 50 = 50. 2 is a factor becaues it gos in to any even number. 5 is a factor becaues 5 × 10 = 50. 10 is a factor becaues it gos into any number that are in ten's place. 25 is a factor becaues if you have two qurtors that would add up to 50. 50 is a factor becaues every number has it self as a factor.*

Donna wrote: *First of all, one has to be a factor, because 1 and itself are always factors of a number. 50 is an even number so 2 is also a factor. 5 is a factor because 50 ends in 0 and 5 × 10 = 50. I just said why 10 is a factor. 50 is*

Factors of 50

① 50=1,2,5,10,25,50

1 is a factor becaues 1×50=60

2 is a Factor becaues it gos in to any even number

5 is a factor becaues 5×10=50

10 is a factor becaues it gos into any number that are in ten's place.

25 is a factor becaues if you have two gurtors that would add up to 50?

50 is a factor becaues every number has it self as a factor.

Nathan carefully explained why 1, 2, 5, 10, 25, and 50 were factors of 50.

FACTORS OF 50

1, 2, 5, 10, 25, 50

I know that numbers 1, 2, 5, 10, 25, 50 are factors of 50 because 1x50 equals 50 and 25x2 equals 50 and 10x5 equals 50 and 5x10 equals 50 2x25 equals 50 50x1 equal 50 and that's why I know that 1, 2, 5, 10, 25, 50 are factors and the all equal 50.

an even number and $\frac{1}{2}$ of it is 25. Then of course, there's 50. When I was explaining 1 I told you why 50 must also be a factor. The number itself is always its highest factor, so that was as far as I could go.

Shane explained how he knew he had all of the factors for 50: *Once you get half way* [25] *no number can fit in it. That's how I kwon* [know] *how to find them all.*

"Can you explain your thinking a little more, Shane?" I asked.

"Well, 1, 2, 5, and 10, and 25 are factors of 50," he explained. "I know that 25 is half way to 50 and there are no more factors of 50 past 25 except for 50 itself."

Throughout the week, the students worked on an extension of the activity by investigating the numbers from 51 to 100. We continued to discuss how we were sure we had found all the ways to count to each number. We also made predictions about which numbers between 1 and 100 would have the most factors.

From a Fourth Grade Class

Shelley Ferguson's fourth graders had been studying about multiplication and had also built rectangular arrays for the numbers from 1 to 36. The students had represented the arrays on a class chart using graph paper.

After reading aloud *Two Ways to Count to Ten*, Shelley posed a problem. "The antelope had to count to 10," she began, "but suppose the antelope had to count to 24? How many ways are there to count to 24?"

Shelley tried to help her students make a connection between skip counting and the rectangular arrays they had made. "Look at the rectangular arrays," Shelley said, "and see if the arrays can help you count to a number."

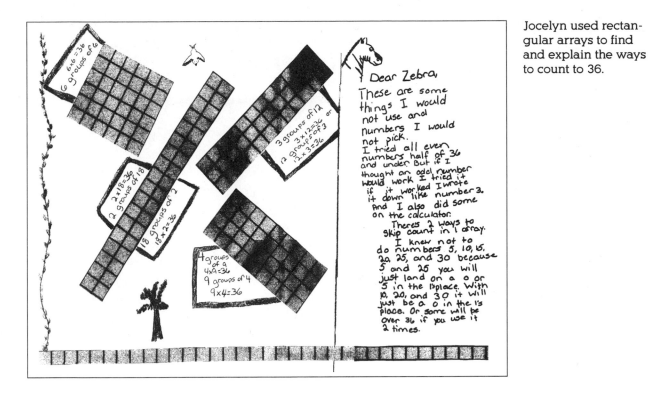

Jocelyn used rectangular arrays to find and explain the ways to count to 36.

The students worked on this problem in a variety of ways. Some used calculators, some skip counted by 2s, 3s, 8s, and 12s, and some students used square tiles to make different rectangular arrays.

When the students figured out the ways to count to 24, Shelley posed a similar problem. "What are the ways to count to 36?" she asked. "How can you find all the ways? How will you know when you've found them all?"

Shelley asked her students to explain their reasoning by writing a letter to the antelope (or another animal) to suggest ways to count to 36.

Cassidy wrote: *Dear Lion, I think you should count by 12's to 36 because it's quick. I do not think you should count by 18's or 36's because someone could acoue* [accuse] *you of cheating.*

From a Sixth Grade Class

Suzanne McGrath's sixth graders had just completed a unit on factors and multiples when she read *Two Ways to Count to Ten*. Her sixth graders listened attentively to the story and investigated the factors for each number from 1 to 100.

The following week, Suzanne began a unit on geometry. When they were studying angles, one of Suzanne's students asked, "Why do circles have 360 degrees?"

"I don't know," Suzanne replied, "but I think I know where we can look for the answer."

Suzanne brought to class the book *Circles,* by Katherine Sheldrick Ross. This book explores the history of different geometric shapes—circles, spheres, cylinders, cones, and others. The book also offers interesting activities for children ages 8 to 14.

Suzanne turned to page 37 and read to her class about why circles have 360 degrees. Her students were fascinated to learn that the ancient Babylonians based their number system on 60 and that they were the ones who decided to divide a circle into 360 equal parts. They chose 360 because it's divisible by so many whole numbers.

"How many numbers divide evenly into 360?" Suzanne asked. Suzanne reported that this problem was a perfect extension to *Two Ways to Count to Ten.* She added that it was also a nice way to connect one topic of mathematics with another.

Factors of 360

1, 2, 3, 6, 10, 12, 20, 30, 45, 60, 90, 120, 180, 360

• 1 because 1 is a factor of every whole number.
• 2 because the last digit is an even number, 0.
• 3 & 6 because 6 & 3 is are factors of 30 (x 2=60) and factors of 300 (30 x 10).
• 10 because every number that has the last digit being a zero is in 1 x 10 = or 5 x 10 = so forth
• 12 & 120 because 12 x 3 = 36 x 10 = 360 or 120 x 3 = 360
• 20 because any number that ends in 0 and has tens digit being even can be divided by 20.
• 30 because 30 x 2 = 60 plus 30 x 10 = 300 = 360
• 45 & 90 because we're studying angles and 45 is half of 90 which is ¼ of 360.
• 60 because 60 times 3 = 180 x 2 = 360
• 180 because in angles 180 is half of the circle (360)
• 360 because 360 + 0 = 360 or 360 x 1 = 360, it's the number we're looking for.

Lesley explained how she found all the factors for 360.

Roll Two Dice

2	3	4	5	6	7	8	9	10	11	12

Finish Line

Postal Rate History

The chart below shows the cost to mail a 1-ounce First Class letter in the United States since 1917. Based on the information in the chart, predict the cost of mailing a 1-ounce First Class letter in 2001. Explain your reasoning.

November 3, 1917 . . . . 3 cents

July 1, 1919 . . . . 2 cents

July 6, 1932 . . . . 3 cents

August 1, 1958 . . . . 4 cents

January 7, 1963 . . . . 5 cents

January 7, 1968 . . . . 6 cents

May 16, 1971 . . . . 8 cents

March 2, 1974 . . . . 10 cents

December 31, 1975 . . . . 13 cents

May 29, 1978 . . . . 15 cents

March 22, 1981 . . . . 18 cents

November 1, 1981 . . . . 20 cents

February 17, 1985 . . . . 22 cents

April 3, 1988 . . . . 25 cents

February 3, 1991 . . . . 29 cents

January 1, 1995 . . . . 32 cents

From *Math and Literature (Grades 4–6)*. © 1995 Math Solutions Publications

BIBLIOGRAPHY

Many of these books are available from:

Cuisenaire Company of America
P.O. Box 5026
White Plains, NY 10602-5026
(800) 237-3142

Anno, Mitsumasa. *Anno's Magic Seeds.* Philomel Books, 1995.

Barry, David. *The Rajah's Rice.* Illustrated by Donna Perrone. W. H. Freeman, 1994.

Birch, David. *The King's Chessboard.* Illustrated by Devis Grebu. Puffin Pied Piper Books, 1988.

Briggs, Raymond. *Jim and the Beanstalk.* Coward-McCann, Inc., 1970.

Chwast, Seymour. *The Twelve Circus Rings.* Gulliver Books/Harcourt Brace Jovanovich, 1993.

Clement, Rod. *Counting on Frank.* Gareth Stevens Publishing, 1991.

Dahl, Roald. *Esio Trot.* Illustrated by Quentin Blake. Viking Penguin, 1990.

Dee, Ruby. *Two Ways to Count to Ten.* Illustrated by Susan Meddaugh. Holt, Rinehart & Winston, 1988.

Ernst, Lisa Campbell. *Sam Johnson and the Blue Ribbon Quilt.* Mulberry Books, 1983.

Frasier, Debra. *On the Day You Were Born.* Harcourt Brace Jovanovich, 1991.

Giganti, Paul, Jr. *Each Orange Had 8 Slices.* Illustrated by Donald Crews. Greenwillow Books, 1992.

McKissack, Patricia C. *A Million Fish . . . More or Less.* Illustrated by Dena Schutzer. Alfred A. Knopf, 1992.

Milton, Nancy. *The Giraffe that Walked to Paris.* Illustrated by Roger Roth. Crown Publishers, Inc., 1992.

Pinczes, Elinor J. *A Remainder of One.* Illustrated by Bonnie MacKain. Houghton Mifflin Company, 1995.

Pittman, Helena Clare. *A Grain of Rice.* Bantam Skylark, 1986.

Ross, Katherine Sheldrick. *Circles.* Addison-Wesley, 1993.

Rylant, Cynthia. *Mr. Griggs' Work.* Illustrated by Julie Downing. Orchard Books, 1989.

Schwartz, Amy. *Annabelle Swift, Kindergartner.* Orchard Books, 1988.

Shannon, George. *Stories to Solve: Folk Tales from Around the World.* Beech Tree Books, 1991.

Sharmat, Marjorie Weinman. *The 329th Friend.* Illustrated by Cyndy Szekeres. Four Winds Press, 1979.

Tahan, Malba. *The Man Who Counted: A Collection of Mathematical Adventures.* Translated by Leslie Clark and Alastair Reid. Illustrated by Patricia Reid Baquero. W. W. Norton & Company, 1993.

Tompert, Ann. *Grandfather Tang's Story.* Illustrated by Robert Andrew Parker. Crown Publishers, 1990.

Van Allsburg, Chris. *Jumanji.* Houghton Mifflin, 1981.

Wells, Robert E. *Is a Blue Whale the Biggest Thing There Is?* Albert Whitman & Company, 1993.

INDEX